FUELLING THE FIRE
FRESH THINKING ON PRAYER

DENNIS LENNON

Scripture Union, 207–209 Queensway, Bletchley, MK2 2EB, England, UK
Email: info@scriptureunion.org.uk
Website: www.scriptureunion.org.uk

ISBN: 1 84427 149 8

Scripture Union Australia
Locked Bag 2, Central Coast Business Centre, NSW 2252
www.su.org.au

First published in the U.K. by Scripture Union, 2005

British Library Cataloguing-in-Publication data
A catalogue record for this book is available from the British Library.

Cover design: ie design, Birmingham

Internal design and typesetting by Servis Filmsetting Ltd, Manchester

Printed in Great Britain by Creative Print and Design, Ebbw Vale, Wales

Scripture Union is an international Christian charity working with churches in
more than 130 countries, providing resources to bring the good news about Jesus
Christ to children, young people and families and to encourage them to develop
spiritually through the Bible and prayer.
As well as our network of volunteers, staff and associates who run holidays,
church-based events and school Christian groups, we produce a wide range of
publications and support those who use our resources through training
programmes.

CONTENTS

Contents

Chapter 1

COORDINATED WITH ETERNITY

Writing about prayer is a perilous business, like a child playing near deep water. For the writer, there is the danger of becoming more concerned with words about prayer than with praying. Equally, the reader risks learning more about prayer, without praying more. For the person who prays there is 'danger' in throwing oneself into the hands of the living God, 'a consuming fire' (Hebrews 12:29); and we tangle with the spiritual principalities and powers of the universe. There is danger also in the way we are scrutinised and evaluated by our own prayer life, for, 'as a man prays, so he is'. Nor do our personal relationships come through exposure to prayer unscathed, for, as we soon discover, praying for others quite alters the way we see them. You could even say that prayer holds 'dangers' for the world, since the petition, 'Your kingdom come, your will be done on earth as in heaven' invites a cataclysmic movement.

At the outset of these reflections, however, we need to come a little closer to home and consider the dangers we may pose to worship and prayer through the scope they allow for self-delusion and hypocrisy.

Prayer ... honestly

In which other aspect of the Christian life is there such wide discrepancy between the glowing things we say (about prayer) and the dismal realities of our practice? We are an open book to our Lord Jesus, who targeted our love of play-acting and directed that we pray out of sight, alone with our heavenly Father (Matthew

6:6), because intention and motive are everything in our relationship with him. Of course we pray corporately, with other people as well, but the integrity of our prayer life, the vital prayer-without-pretending, will only be established when we are alone with the Father. Prayer with any ulterior motive of self-promotion is as disgraceful as a man buying his wife a gift and telling the neighbour how much he paid for it. In the name of transparency and sincerity we could usefully install a warning device in that part of the brain where desires and motivations are formed, which would flash and bleep whenever we stray too close to fantasy in the things we say about our prayer.

I like the refreshing and challenging honesty of this observation: 'Prayer for many is like a foreign land. When we go there, we go as tourists. Like most tourists, we feel uncomfortable and out of place. Like most tourists we move on before too long and go somewhere else.'[1] That, unfortunately, has the ring of truth; it is a disturbing acknowledgement that we are so soon ill at ease with the One who is the source of all life. Gerard Manley Hopkins grasped our utter dependence upon God for every moment's existence:

> Thee God, I come from, to thee go,
> All day long I like fountain flow
> From thy hand out, swayed about
> Mote-like in thy mighty glow.[2]

In that vision the response of wondering gratitude for life caught up in God's wisdom and power is unforced and natural, like breathing, as much to be expected as the dazzle caused by bright sunlight on water. The dazzle isn't added afterwards for aesthetic effect; neither is the spirit of praise in us an optional extra, turned on whenever are we in the mood. This incredible instrument of our bodily self is created for praise; God's works and our minds are mutually attuned.

'Faith without deeds is dead', wrote James (2:26), and the first deed, the source of all spiritual activity, is prayer.

Hopkins' image of life, our life, as streaming out through God's hands and playfully thrown around, 'swayed about', as in a spontaneous, original dance 'mote-like in thy mighty glow', follows the contours of Paul's doxology:

> For from him and through him and to him are all things.
> To him be the glory for ever! Amen.
>
> Romans 11:36

Sin, therefore, is the negation of prayer and worship. The effect of sin is to shatter the instrument, to gag the voice, to deface the music; sin is blank. Redemption restores the song, as George Herbert beautifully expressed:

> Man is out of order hurl'd,
> Parcell'd out to all the world,
> Lord, thy broken consort raise,
> And the music shall be praise.[3]

Augustine gives a picture of personal life homing in towards God as a compass needle swings around searching for magnetic north. Life moves towards fulfilment by celebrating (in as many ways as imagination can invent) the beauty, truth, love and goodness of God:

> Can any praise be worthy of the Lord's majesty? How magnificent his strength! How incredible his wisdom! Man is one of your creatures Lord, and his instinct is to praise you . . . since he is part of your creation, he wishes to praise you. The thought of you stirs him so deeply that he cannot be content unless he praises you, because you made us for yourself and our hearts find no peace unless they rest in you.[4]

God's joy (the joy which he has as God, and the joy he bestows on us) is the organising principle at the heart of the cosmos. Whenever we take time to make something not out of necessity but for the pleasure of it, we are being true to our image-of-God nature. He creates for the sheer joy of sharing himself with his creation. In response, our joy bursts through into prayer spoken

9

and lived, which move in harmony with God's joy; it is then that we are at our best.

As the life of the Holy Trinity ecstatically overflows into creation, our thought, love and language, and our music and powers of expression may have to burst their banks in an attempt to keep pace with what we are witnessing in a world 'charged with the grandeur of God'.[5] Look, listen, study, touch and feel the beauty, power and wisdom of God, and then allow it to lead you out into worship. John Donne looked forward to the transformations of the next life when he would no longer struggle to make music for God but 'I shall be made thy music'. In that vision the present life is preparation for the real performances to come, therefore

> . . . as I come
> I tune the instrument here at the door,
> And what I must do then, think now before.[6]

Whether or not that great theologian PT Forsyth was correct in his opinion that 'the worst sin is prayerlessness', it is beyond question true that neglect of prayer is a supreme folly. For if, as Christians claim, prayer is nothing less than living with God and God living with us, then its neglect constitutes a bizarre form of self-damage, like someone ill choosing to live in outer Siberia instead of the Spice Islands. To allow ourselves to descend into feeble 'tourism-prayer' is to mislay, carelessly, the pearl of great value (Matthew 13:45,46). The shift out of tourist mode, into the biblical attitudes of the true settler who inhabits, cultivates, defends and delights in the boundless spaces of prayer territory, is one of the concerns of this book.

But we must probe a little further into what gives rise to the malaise which makes prayer feel like a visit 'to a foreign land'. Put bluntly, why is it that so many of us seem allergic to prayer beyond an elementary level?

You become what you breathe

When I worked in a coal-mining region of the country, coming in as an outsider I was struck by the effects mining had on the population's health in respiratory disorders. On that analogy, perhaps our unease with prayer can be traced to the air we breathe. We must take action to guard against the spiritual pollutants pumped out by a prevailing culture which is atheistic, materialistic, hedonistic, and cynical. Ignore the dangers, and respiratory difficulties will follow inevitably (doesn't it strike you that the church seems, somehow, 'out of breath'?). Consider how the spirit of the present time can infiltrate and erode our desire for the presence of God.

First, a pervasive secular scepticism colonises minds by a process of stealthy osmosis. We hardly know it's happening until it has happened and, one morning, we wake up dead. One sure sign that we have expired will be prayerlessness, or at least boredom at the thought of praying – a failing joy and energy in worship, the sense that prayer is now an uncomfortable visit to a foreign place. What will have brought on this crisis? Desperate to discredit God through a prayerless or merely 'tourist' church, demonic powers work through a hostile secularism to subvert Christian claims that prayer in Christ's name results in the blessings Christ promised. You are familiar with the sweet reasonableness of the approach: 'It's a free country, so by all means go ahead and pray if you like; worship if it makes you feel better, only whatever you do don't for a moment think that it makes any difference to life in the real world.' Atheism's objection is that God is the self-projection of the one praying. Thus the holy dialogue which is prayer addressed to 'Our Father', is gutted and reduced to a lonely monologue, a futile 'churning the void to make butter'.

There is nothing new in this process. For Jesus, the great question mark over his church concerned its possible loss of faith. In reply to his disciples' insecurities, he said they should have no doubt about God's willingness to answer prayer, but 'when the Son of Man comes, will he find faith on the earth?' (Luke 18:8) or will he find a faith drained of vitality, a tourist-prayer sort of faith? The writer to the Hebrews powerfully raised the same possibility by a different metaphor: 'We must pay more careful attention, therefore, to what we have heard, so that we do not *drift away*' (Hebrews 2:1). A colourful phrase, used also of a boat eased from its moorings by the pull of the tide, and of a ring accidentally slipping off a finger. It suggests a gradual surrender to external influences; bit-by-bit, moment-by-moment, day-by-day, imperceptibly until boat, or ring, or Christian is lost. Paul called the same process conforming 'to the pattern of this world', for which the only protection is to go on the offensive and seek from the Holy Spirit transformation 'by the renewing of your mind' (Romans 12:2). Hebrews 2:1 points the way to that renewal through paying 'more careful attention . . . to what we have heard'.

In another chapter we shall look more closely at the vital connection between the word which God speaks to us out of Scripture, and our answering prayer. For the moment you might consider the remark that Wallace Stevens made about the power of the memorised word. In fact he was referring to poetry, but his insight is even more valid when the word is God's Word. He said that the memorised word creates 'a violence within that protects us from a violence without'.[7] The seemingly inescapable and irresistible swarms of images, words and messages in our environment are mostly designed and propagated with the intention of slipping under our radar, to enter and alter our perceptions. Unless there is a counter-violence within our minds, which pushes back against the incoming violence, we will, for sure one day wake up faithless and prayerless. We must deliberately set out to pre-possess our minds and imaginations with God's living and active Word (Hebrews 4:12).

Jesus went further, teaching that what comes out of the mouth (including prayer) comes first out of the heart; therefore take great care, for 'Good people bring good things out of the good stored up in their hearts . . . For out of the overflow of one's heart the mouth speaks' (Luke 6:45). When did you last 'store up in your heart' the good, faith-building, prayer-inspiring word of God, such that it 'overflowed' from your mouth?

A second attack on faith and prayer derives from the spirit of individualism characteristic of our society.

Prayer and the DIY fallacy

Several days ago I attended a prayer meeting for church leaders in preparation for a week of Bible ministry. The man who led the gathering opened with a prayer in which he called on the Lord to 'come among us'. Perhaps that was a slip of the tongue, but it spoke volumes. According to that request, prayer is something we do and into which we invite the Lord. But that view of prayer is deeply flawed through our terminal self-reliance, with its inevitable consequences of exhaustion and, eventually, despair.

We admire self-reliance and initiative; some of my best friends are never happier than when struggling with an IKEA flat-pack. We admire those individuals who appear to go through life with a list of skills to master: today, motorbike maintenance; tomorrow, Burmese cuisine; next day, snake charming. They are an inspiration, if a discomforting challenge to one's own idleness.

Self-improvement is a magnificent instinct and thoroughly Christian (Matthew 25:14–23), but when, as in our society, God is largely removed from personal calculations, he is replaced by the self, and the cult of the self. An example: there are on the shelves of the bookshops in the US over 700 different titles each containing the word 'self'. Books on self-help, self-esteem, maximise the self, self-realisation, etc etc; hundreds of that ilk, in a breathless, boundless celebration of the self. It suggests a narcissistic culture mesmerised by the power, authority and autonomy of the self, and if I mention the situation in the US it is only because it holds up a mirror to what is happening here.

The point is this: to the DIY mentality, in a society that revolves around the 'self', prayer becomes just one more skill to be mastered. Notice how the thought develops: I regard prayer as something I initiate in response to the Lord's invitation. Prayer happens when I pray and ceases when I stop. My room is silent until I start praying out loud, and falls silent again when I've finished. Clearly prayer is something *we* do and if we fail to do it, prayer for starving people in Sudan, or for the friend in the next road, doesn't happen. We accept it as our duty to crank

13

the prayer mill endlessly in obedience to the Lord's command. If this is a fair description of our attitudes towards prayer, as essentially depending on us, no wonder it becomes such a wearisome business. (We distinguish here between the authentic burden of prayer, and prayer as plain burdensome.)

To return to that prayer meeting and the impression that it was our gathering into which we invited the Lord – *in fact the reverse is true*. Long before we arrived, the Lord Jesus was occupying that room, standing before the Father, offering worship and intercession for our Bible week, not only praying *for* his people but *as* his people, for he is our representative, who takes our prayers into his, offered as his. As surely as he saves us from our sins, so also he is ceaselessly saving us from our ineffectual prayer. As we arrived for prayer our first attitude should have been one of realisation and acknowledgement that 'the Lord is here' and at work, for he 'always lives to intercede' for his people (Hebrews 7:25). Next, we should have allowed the Holy Spirit to cleanse and attune our minds to the frequency of Christ's mind, so that we enter into Christ's worship. In this vision of prayer the key word is not 'initiate' but 'participate' in the prayer Jesus offers. Clearly we must look more closely at this marvellous truth (in a further chapter). The point to stress for now is that worship and prayer are the Lord's feast. They are going on at this moment, just as they have been ever since his resurrection; and we are invited to join in.

We are not alone. Jesus is praying and we enter into his prayer and worship, and even that is far from the full picture. Our praying begins with Christ and among the glorious angelic beings, who are wonderfully accomplished in adoration since the beginning of creation. We are not alone, and again we are mistaken to imagine that prayer only happens when *we* decide to pray. All creation prays! But, because of our incorrigible preoccupation with our own initiatives, we feel isolated and solitary, struggling to get prayer going, speaking our words into the void. God gives us the company of angels and before we have put a sentence together the cosmos is already rocking on its axis at their praise. 'You have come to thousands upon thousands of angels in joyful assembly' (Hebrews 12:22) is true of the present moment, not only when we die. Another version gives, 'we have come before countless angels making festival'.

Boundary people, horizon people

The great prophet meditating in the temple glimpsed just a fraction of that scene, and it frightened him out of his wits (Isaiah 6:1–4). The truth about us at prayer is that we are as much in heaven, among angels and in the presence of God, as we are in the world and in the presence of our neighbours. We are a boundary people, horizon people, standing (or kneeling) between heaven and earth. In Helmut Thielieke's fine phrase we are 'coordinated with eternity',[8] and it follows that if we are coordinated with eternity we dare not allow ourselves to be harassed or hounded by time.

To the great impoverishment of our prayer life, we remain for the most part stubbornly secular in our attitudes towards angels. As a consequence, our environment and atmosphere feel 'empty' and we are thrown back onto our own devices as we try to work up a sense of heaven. The way the devotional kitsch industry has caricatured angels has blighted our spiritual imagination, as a stroll through your local churchyard will illustrate: all those sweet, inoffensive, swooning 'angels' with such inadequate wingspans! If we follow clues given in Revelation 8 and 10, we will be more inclined to believe CS Lewis' hair-raising description of angels as, 'a tornado of sheer monstrosities . . . Darting pillars filled with eyes, lightening pulsations of flame, talons and beaks and billowy masses of what suggests snow, volleyed through cubes and heptagons into an infinite black void'.[9] Imagine praying in an environment with such astounding beings, God's servants, on our side, for, 'Are not all angels ministering spirits sent to serve those who will inherit salvation?' (Hebrews 1:14).

Returning to the vision of Revelation 8, we witness the divine response to the prayers of the church. The angel has scooped

15

blazing coals into his censer from the great altar, he whirls it around his head to fan the fire, and tosses the blazing contents onto the earth and onto the heads of Christ's enemies. The resulting pandemonium is described in classic apocalyptic pyrotechnics, 'peals of thunder, rumblings, flashes of lightning and an earthquake' (v 5). It is a dazzling portrayal of what goes on in heaven, and then on earth, when Christians pray. So much for ideas of prayer as a private, serene, soothing, palliative activity!

When she prays, the church moves from the margins of affairs (local, national and international) to their centre, the place where the outcomes are decided. Thus a numerically tiny, anonymous, socially and politically 'irrelevant' company of people are in the thick of the action. Indeed, those Christians initiate the action by their praying; they are the aggressors, setting the earth ablaze with the dangerous, cleansing fires of God's purposes.

We are too inclined to regard prayer as a kind of spiritual fire-engine, which we wheel out in reaction to crises, in an attempt to dampen down the fires of satanic activity in society. The truth is rather the reverse. Praying Christians are the arsonists as they bring their requests to the throne, mingled with angelic incense, requesting that God's will be done on earth as it is in heaven. Praying believers are the fire-raisers, and it is the godless powers infiltrating political, social and economic structures who struggle to douse the conflagrations of God's prayer-answering action in the world.

'However, when the Son of Man comes will he find faith on earth?'

Questions for reflection and discussion

1. 'Life moves towards fulfilment by celebrating (in as many ways as imagination can invent) the beauty, truth, love and goodness of God' (p 9). What fresh expressions of praise has your imagination invented recently?
2. Do you agree with the theologian PT Forsyth that 'the worst sin is prayerlessness?' (p 10).

3. Read Revelation 8:1–5.
   'Christians initiate the action by their praying; they are the aggressors, setting the earth ablaze with the dangerous fires of God . . . the arsonists . . . the fire-raisers' (p 16).
   Does your own church at prayer reflect such a view? Or is it more like 'a visit to a foreign land?' (p 10).
4. 'You become what you breathe' (p 10). How can a Christian avoid breathing 'the spiritual pollutants pumped out by the prevailing culture'?

Chapter 2

THE BONFIRE

Pondering the stupendous energies in creation, an awestruck Gerard Manley Hopkins exclaimed, 'Million fuelled, nature's bonfire burns on'.[1] Christians also look at the world and marvel at another bonfire, of universal worship and prayer. What fuels it? A thoughtful visitor from Mars looking into the past century of our world's history might be astonished that prayer and praise had not vanished off the face of our earth. He could cite the horrors of our times: catastrophic world wars and countless vicious smaller ones; crazed tyrants in Europe and the Far East, titanic Marxist systems appearing like the antichrist in the former USSR and China; mass terror, demonic cruelties between peoples; holocaust, genocide, persecution; the hellish list goes on and on, conjuring images of the locusts from the Abyss which sting like scorpions but have human faces (Revelation 9:1–7).

In our own society, hostility to vital faith has, so far, been of a different sort, subtler but hardly less lethal. The 'isms' are stacked against serious Christian commitment: sophisticated atheism in influential places (particularly the media); materialism; scientism; relativism; neo-Darwinism; rampant consumerism and unbridled hedonism; all lower the spiritual temperature to arctic levels. Our Martian friend might well wonder how active faith in the God of love could possibly survive such a climate. Yet, like miraculous flowers pushing up through the permafrost (or does the bonfire melt the permafrost?), countless believing people emerge from the darkness and the cold, still trusting God, still worshipping him, unsubjugated by the enemy. As for Marxism, you will find it gathering dust in the museum of failed utopias. How does the great bonfire of prayer and worship burn on and on? What, or who, fuels it?

A fire not ours

People refer to prayer as an instinct as natural and as compelling as breathing; it is an upward urge of the soul; it is a sense of reaching beyond the claustrophobic confines of the present moment to touch the heart of things in God. But still we ask, what fuels the instinct, the urge, the sense? At this point two answers appear, one practical the other theological. You are familiar with the practical answer, which works on Hudson Taylor's maxim that in God's service 'things look up when looked after'. So, sack the present music group and get a better one; and while you are at it get a better sound system, and improve the lighting for the organist; a more reliable 'power-point' would help and you might reposition the choir and worship group nearer to the congregation, and ask the choir to dress informally instead of wearing those robes.

If this answer sounds just too banal, drop in on worship post-mortems up and down the land of a Sunday. Of course, higher standards of performance and presentation matter, and because we are all affected by moods and atmospheres, by all means let's have uplifting ones. Similarly with prayer: a warm room in the middle of winter is more conducive to prayer than a chilly, unfriendly one. There are things that can and should be done, but when all is done these considerations hardly reflect Scripture's understanding of worship, and what fuels the bonfire. After all, secular organisations will also pay close and skilled attention to the practicalities of their public events.

The second answer is theological. Scripture teaches that worship and prayer, as with the totality of Christian life, derive from the Godhead, the Father, Son and Holy Spirit. More commonly today, the third person of the Trinity, the Spirit, is credited almost exclusively, it seems, with the work of empowering, inspiring and renewing spiritual life and especially worship; but Scripture has more to say and rejects the current tendency to distort the activity of the Holy Spirit into an unbridled 'spiritism'. The bonfire of adoration and prayer burns on because it is 'Godhead fuelled'. The Father and the Son are as involved as the Holy Spirit. The dynamic of true prayer is born out of Trinitarian life, exchanged in the flow of love between the divine persons. Therefore, our reflections in this chapter must be about *the resources within the Godhead* which fuel worship.

> Certainly the Christian God, as the revelation of Jesus Christ shows him to us, is almighty, and so he is infinitely rich. But what form does his infinite wealth take? God the Father, the origin of everything, gives away himself and all that he is and has to his only begotten Son, who in turn does not store up all this treasure within himself but acknowledges it as the Father's gift and returns it to him; these Two by no means stay enclosed in a kind of mutual egoism but, in mutual selflessness, cause the Holy Spirit to proceed from them, the Spirit of absolute love, the epitome of eternal wealth in this unceasing exchange of gifts. Even though God's triune nature remains a profound mystery, we can grasp this: In God, power and wealth are not qualities existing side by side with love and external to it; they are identical with it. God only *has* in so far as he *gives*, and this giving is of his innermost essence.[2]

For an instance of biblical teaching on this insight, look at Jesus' words in his great high-priestly prayer in which he adores the Father for the giving and receiving of life and glory between the two of them, in the Holy Spirit.

> Father, the time has come. Glorify your Son, that your Son may glorify you . . . I have brought you glory on earth by completing the work you gave me to do. And now, Father, glorify me in your presence with the glory I had with you before the world began.
>
> I have revealed you to those whom you gave me out of the world. They were yours; you gave them to me and they have obeyed your

word. Now they know that everything you have given me comes from you . . . All I have is yours, and all you have is mine.

John 17:1–10

To summarise: the Father pours out honour and glory to the Son; the Son pours himself out in worship of the Father; the Spirit, who is the Spirit of Glory, flows between Father and Son, and out into creation. Notice also the astonishing honour done to ourselves as we are drawn into the giving and receiving between Father and Son. In fact *we* are the treasured gifts which are exchanged between them (a startling insight into what goes on in evangelism).

Visualising the doctrine

How do you picture to yourself the doctrine of the Trinity as we have so far sketched it? Doctrine remains at arm's length, abstract, on the page, until we 'see' it as we visualise it to ourselves. So what do you 'see' as you ponder the life between the Father, Son and the Spirit in their mutually glorifying flow of love and gifts?

One visualisation, which has fed the faith-imagination of Christians for the past thousand years, sees the divine persons moving in an ecstatic dance, the 'Perichoresis' ('circular dance') on God's cosmic village green. The richness, the ravishing beauty and the sheer encouragement in the metaphor, and its attempt to represent faithfully the scriptural revelation, has delighted and informed Christians in their attempts to understand the Trinity, since the tenth century (John of Damascus is credited with its appearance).

The Perichoresis is the dance of pure selflessness, the self-giving of Father to Son, and Son to Father in the Holy Spirit. As the dance moves and turns through the cosmos and through time, the Father approaches the Son with expressions of out-pouring in honour of the Son. The Son receives the Father's gifts with joy and gratitude; then, in the dance, he moves towards the

Father with gestures of adoring submission to his will. The Spirit of love and glory flows between Father and Son, available to both, ministering to both.

With the Perichoresis in mind, consider what Scripture means by saying we are 'in Christ' and Christ is 'in us' (Colossians 2:9,10; 3:1–4, 11) and that we are thereby 'in the Father'; and such mutual indwelling between ourselves and the Godhead is real because we are in the Holy Spirit and the Spirit is in us (Ephesians 2:18; 1 Corinthians 2:10–15; 2 Corinthians 3:18; Colossians 3:10; John 14:23). To be 'in God' and 'God in us' implies that, with utterly astounding grace, the Trinity have opened the dance to us also. The divine persons turn towards us, opening the circle for us to enter. How do you visualise the scene? Our approach to God in prayer and worship, and our expectations of what might be happening at that moment, are largely determined by the images we carry around deep in the imagination. One thing is for sure: the Perichoresis demolishes those rigid, fixed and static visualisations of our relationship with God; pictures which have bullied and oppressed the imaginations of too many of us for too long. The Dance suggests rather that we have plunged into and are immersed within a torrent of love and delight, a cascading river of the divine self-outpouring as Father, Son and Spirit give glory to each other without any holding back (Psalm 36:8,9). In the Cosmic Dance of pure love, 'God only *has* as far as he *gives*, and this giving is of his innermost essence.' Within the Dance, we are bathed in the immensities of God's kindness and generosity as his love flows around and over us. There we glimpse the riches of his self-giving.

Each of us must decide what to do with this doctrine. We have tried to visualise it, and to see our own place in the midst of the Perichoresis, but how will it affect us and our practice of prayer and worship? There is the danger that we will filter the Dance and its thrilling interpretation of our life with the Trinity, through the cynicism of a culture that has lost its spiritual nerve; it finds the Perichoresis just too much to take, it is far too staggeringly exotic, just too marvellous to be true (some of this attitude lingers around in the churches also, where contemporary culture has taken over the mind of the congregation). Or will we yield to the vision of life as participating in the playful, ecstatic joy of the Godhead, as the reality by which all else is tested? One thing the Perichoresis makes clear beyond question: the love and generosity which is the essence of God is also at the centre of his creation – its origin, its reason for being and its goal, since, 'the whole earth is full of his glory' (Isaiah 6:3).

Making connections

'Godhead fuelled, prayer's bonfire burns on.' What difference will this truth make? First, that the God we come to in our weakness and with our many fears and requests is the God who exists to give himself away without ever exhausting his generosity, 'more than all we ask or imagine' (Ephesians 3:20). Our intercessions merely supply more scope for his generosity towards our world. It is obvious that with God everything is gift: our creation, preservation, redemption and free access to the Father through Jesus the Son. This demands radical alteration in some of our attitudes. The old pagan insecurities, the indecisiveness and hesitations, the suspicions, the coolness in our approach to the Father, really cannot survive within the Perichoresis – so be done with them once and for all (and again tomorrow!)

Other consequences follow as a result of the Dance. We are endowed with a totally new status, and therefore a new confidence with the Father. Now, at last, we can be free of our customary role as spiritual street urchin, hanging about in the rain outside the Father's great house, looking in through the windows at the lights, the partying, the food and yes, that Dance. Our attitude has been the partly self-pitying and partly self-hating one of 'it isn't for the likes of me'; anyway, if we went in we would only be embarrassed and feel hopelessly out of place. So we have settled for the apologetic tone appropriate for tramps whose place is round at the back door hoping for some leftovers. But the Godhead will not hear of it. The Father deals with all his children by grace and by gift, not according to what people like to call their 'worth'. He explodes the myth of our craven unworthiness (a myth which, in a perverse and sick way, some may even have come to embrace and, dare we say, enjoy), and insists we come in, for his home is our home (Grace! Gift!) and enter the Dance (Luke 15:22–24).

Now our requests can be large, for the Father's generosity is immense and he delights in our company within Trinitarian life. Be open to the sudden surprises that may have little, if anything, to do with our lists of requests. No longer will we shuffle to prayer with the fidgeting unease of the nervous visitor to a foreign land whose language and customs he does not understand (see p 8) – by grace and by gift, we belong here! Put his address at the top of the notepaper: your home is within the unfolding life of the Godhead. Perhaps it is inconsistent of us to continue speaking of '*coming* to prayer' as though we are here and 'prayer' is over there, somewhere. By grace and therefore as a free gift, we are in God, a fact which, said George Herbert, 'makes one place everywhere'. In God we already live in the sphere of communion, the giving and receiving of glory, gifts and blessing. Worship, prayer and intercession are the life of the Perichoresis, and we are *there*. The bonfire burns on and on, because there is no dead distance between prayer and the Trinity; prayer is now our proper, 'natural' environment. We will live through the day with our hearts open to the Father, breathing our praise and prayer and receiving the impressions of his grace. We pray, because it is in God's nature to give and give and then flood our lives with the boundless generosity which is his essence. (The code word for this wonder is 'grace'.) Prayer is like that, because God is like that.

Other immense scriptures are drawn to this theme like moths to a flame (or to a bonfire).

Typically, writing to the Ephesians, Paul extols the resources which are the Godhead and which fuel prayer and worship:

Praise be to the God and Father of our Lord Jesus Christ, who has blessed us in the heavenly realms with every spiritual blessing in Christ.

. . . to the praise of his glorious grace, which he has freely given us in the One he loves . . . he made known to us the mystery of his will according to his good pleasure, which he purposed in Christ.

Ephesians 1:3–9

I pray also that the eyes of your heart may be enlightened in order that you may know the hope to which he has called you, the riches of his glorious inheritance in the saints, and his incomparably great power for us who believe. That power is the like the working of his mighty strength, which he exerted in Christ when he raised him from the dead and seated him at his right hand in the heavenly realms, far above all rule and authority, power and dominion, and every title that can be given, not only in the present age but also in the one to come. And God placed all things under his feet . . .

Ephesians 1:18–22

For through him we both have access to the Father by one Spirit.

Ephesians 2:18

Now to him who is able to do immeasurably more than all we ask or imagine, according to his power that is at work within us, to him be glory in the church and in Christ Jesus throughout all generations, for ever and ever! Amen.

Ephesians 3:20,21

When writing to the Colossians, Paul gives classic expression to our place within the life of the Godhead:

To the holy and faithful brothers and sisters in Christ at Colosse . . .

Colossians 1:2

For he has rescued us from the dominion of darkness and brought us into the kingdom of the Son he loves, in whom we have redemption, the forgiveness of sins.

Colossians 1:13,14

> . . . the glorious riches of this mystery, which is Christ in you, the
> hope of glory.
>
> Colossians 1:27

> For in Christ all the fulness of the Deity lives in bodily form, and you
> have been given fulness in Christ, who is the Head over every power
> and authority.
>
> Colossians 2:9,10

> Since, then, you have been raised with Christ, set your hearts on
> things above, where Christ is seated on the right hand of God . . .
> When Christ, who is your life, appears, then you also will appear with
> him in glory.
>
> Colossians 3:1–4

Immersed in fullness

Out of the riches of the Godhead we are, above all else, people
who pray. First, in adoration of the Father. But however does one
say 'thank you' for the inestimable privilege of entrance into the
life of the Godhead? By enjoyment. The sincerest form of thanks
is enjoyment. When guests thank my wife for her hospitality what
she really wants to know is, 'have you enjoyed it?'

In this chapter we have been piling up expressions of the Holy
Trinity's stunning hospitality towards us, and we would like to
express our gratitude but we haven't the words. All the Father
wishes to know is 'are you enjoying it?', which will be thanks
enough. Peter was astonished at Christians who 'though you
have not seen him [Christ], you love him; and even though you
do not see him now, you believe in him and are filled with an inexpressible and glorious joy, for you are receiving the goal of your
faith, the salvation of your souls' (1 Peter 1:8,9). There we feel we
are in the presence of people whose bonfire of praise is fuelled by
the Godhead.

Towards God, we respond with a life of grateful thanksgiving.
It is well worth listening once more to Balthasar on this theme:

'The Christian is a child of God, sharing in the divine nature, immersed in the breathtaking fullness and superabundance of God through Christ. Unlike the old Adam, he does not need to scratch around in the poor, cursed soil in order to gather together his bit of wealth and make it a tolerably comfortable living; the entire contents of God's treasure house are poured out at his feet. He does not need to pursue a thirsty search for love and hope; they are infused into him in all the fullness and purity with which they spring from God's source. He is rich beyond measure; fullness is his element; it is within him and forms his whole background. His ethical action is nothing other than *eucharistia*, the gratitude that necessarily follows from this fullness of grace. He can do no other than extol God's benefits; he can do no other than be radiant, since God has set him afire; he cannot but speak, because God has put the word into his mouth; he cannot but pour himself out, together with Christ, into the world's emptiness and poverty, because God has filled him with a richness that is beyond this world, a richness that comes from heaven.

In fact it would be disgraceful if, having been given everything, he were to act as if he were still needy and wretched, still full of demands, still 'toiling and striving'. But it would also be a disgrace if he wanted to keep his unimaginable wealth to himself, to stockpile it like a capitalist and not pour it out for others in thankfulness of heart; for the treasure within him is nothing other than the stream of light that flows from the Godhead'.[3]

Questions for reflection and discussion

1. Do you find the analogy of the Perichoresis, the Dance of the Trinity, helpful? How do you visualise the Trinity fuelling your prayer and your church's worship?
2. 'Each of us must decide what to do with this doctrine' of the Perichoresis (p 21). What are you doing with it? What is it doing with you?

3. 'The Dance suggests rather that we have plunged into and are immersed within a torrent of love and delight, a cascading river of the divine self-outpouring' (p 22).
   For your meditation consider Psalm 36:8,9 with John 7:37–39.
4. 'It would be disgraceful if, having been given everything, he (the child of God) were to act as if he were still needy and wretched, still full of demands, still "toiling and striving"' (p 27). Discuss.

Reflect for a moment on how much of your prayer is asking and how much is thanking.

Chapter 3

PRAYING THE DOCTRINE

We are exploring how knowledge about God translates into praying to God; how his words to us can become our words to him; how he fuels worship, guides prayer and irradiates our communion with him; how we can not only know the doctrine of the Godhead, but also pray it. Or perhaps you regard prayer and doctrine as distant cousins living on separate islands? So, prayer is 'warm, instinctive, spontaneous, sincere, real' while doctrine is 'contrived, bookish, second-hand, cerebral, remote'. But in fact the two are twins, 'Prayer and doctrine are inseparable. They alone can explain each other. Either without the other is meaningless and dead ... No dogma deserves its place unless it is prayable, and no Christian deserves his dogmas, who does not pray them.'[1]

We cannot do better than start where God the Son put words into our heart and mouth for God the Father, in the Lord's Prayer.

Jesus said, This, then, is how you should pray:

> 'Our Father in heaven,
> > hallowed be your name,
> > your kingdom come,
> > your will be done
> > > on earth as it is in heaven.
> > Give us today our daily bread.
> > > Forgive us our debts,
> > > > as we also have forgiven our debtors.

> And lead us not into temptation,
> but deliver us from the evil one.'
>
> Matthew 6:9–13

It may require a great effort of mind to escape the dead hand of overfamiliarity, which tends to domesticate the prayer, reducing it to a cliché. Try to look with fresh eyes and allow the *structure* of the prayer to reach you. The first three of the six petitions are all about God. In this respect, they correspond to the first four Commandments. 'Our Father' opens with his glory. Not about God as our provider, healer, helper, but about himself. In the next chapter we shall explore praying the three petitions – God's name hallowed, his kingdom come, his will done – but in this chapter we stand back a little and regard the three petitions, taken together, as a statement of God's glory, like the colours of the spectrum converging to make white light.

As you think about the shape and the arrangement of the prayer, bring alongside the fact that daily life was, for most in the ancient Near East, an unremitting grind exacerbated by the constant possibility of famine (the kind of 'severe famine in that whole country' that wrecked the prodigal son was not uncommon in the region; Luke 15:14). Imagine also life without anaesthetics. The point is this: given the extent of human need (and nobody observed and responded to it more than Jesus) it seems incredible that he was more concerned with the Father's glory, than with the Father's concern for people's concerns. Yet even as we say such things alarm bells are ringing – there must be more to it.

First tie your knot

By its completely God-ward opening, with nothing and no-one else in the frame, the prayer marks out the order of our approach to the Father. First things first. First God's glory, then our own concerns. Not because God is touchy about his prestige, nor is he threatened by, or jealous of, our need to give so much energy and concentration to life's essentials. It is a matter of how life is set up. If you wish to sew successfully, first tie a knot in your thread. The glory of God is the 'knot'. If you build a house, first lay the foundation. We are saying that the glory of God is the 'foundation'. If you are planning a garden, first check that your patch can see the sun. We are comparing the glory of God to the essential sun. When Hopkins said, 'The world is charged with the grandeur of God', he implied that the rest of us are living off the electricity of God's grandeur. First the supplier, then the consumers; first God, then people. Thus when Jesus says 'seek first his kingdom and his righteousness, and all these things [life's necessities] will be given to you as well' (Matthew 6:33), he is not opposing God's glory to our daily lives, but is making our daily life possible because of God's glory – the knot, foundation, sun and 'electricity' of life.

Jesus isn't asking us to pray for God's glory *instead* of for human need; rather, it is in the deepest nature of creation that life goes best where God is honoured. The creator-wisdom of God has worked a grain into the texture of the world, which runs towards the glory of God as water flows downhill (Colossians 1:16,17). Go with the grain, pray with the grain, and the outcome will be 'right'. But violate the grain, go against or across it, ignoring or despising the primacy of God in creation, and chaos ensues. This isn't open to debate as though it were a matter of opinion, any more than gravity is a question of personal opinion. Put another way, there is only one Author of the play in which we all act. Our part is to respect the authority of the Author, commit to the parts allotted to us, learn our lines and give our best effort to the performance. But we can expect mayhem if the actors dispute the Author's intentions and try to take over the theatre. Where the Father's name, his kingdom and his will, are put first, life flows.

Let me give a warning. We are not relegating ordinary need to the sphere of the unimportant or 'unspiritual'. Petitions four to six establish that people, too, must be given their place: they are not merely so much fodder for the kingdom of God. If we were

31

to omit or diminish four, five and six we would be falling into the error that has troubled the church since its origins, a two-sphere view of life: the one sphere is spiritual, mystical, heavenly, ecclesiastical and theological; the other sphere is to do with work, sex, money, sport, family, food and friends. It is a mischievous split between heaven and earth, which is emphatically rejected by the Lord's Prayer. In Jesus Christ the two spheres are forced together, bound into one, and we pray for both in the one prayer.

'Abba Father'

The very suggestion that God is peeved if not given top billing is exposed for the nonsense it is by the fact that we come to him as 'our Father'. In Jesus' language, Aramaic, the word for Father is 'Abba', which carries the affectionate informality of 'dear Father', or even 'dad'. So precious was this understanding for the writers of the Greek New Testament that at several places they retained the Aramaic 'Abba'; so, too, have our translators into English. In Romans 8:15, where the context is a thrilling affirmation of the Holy Spirit's ministry, Paul urges believers to open their hearts and mouths to call out *'Abba*, Father'. Galatians 4:6 goes further, saying that our hearts are the place into which the Spirit comes, calling out the divine name *'Abba*, Father'. For parents, the first time their child starts to form their name, 'daddy, mummy', is a unique pleasure. Our heavenly Father likewise delights to hear us call to him, 'Abba, Father'. He is no aloof deity, oversensitive about his status, but the self-outpouring 'Abba, Father' of his poor and needy children, even where those children are not yet aware of his love.

Our friend from Mars, observing the tenor of our churches, might with reason conclude that Christians use God for what they can get from him, less interested in him than in his goods. Perhaps our indignation that Jesus gives the Father's glory priority over human needs suggests that this Martian is more perceptive than he looks. In which case, if we are more like God-exploiters than God-adorers, every time we utter the Lord's

Prayer (and personally I seem to use it more, and more urgently, the older I get) could be an opportunity to purge our motives.

In the earliest times of the church not everyone was allowed to pray the Lord's Prayer, only those who were full members. It was treated as 'one of the most holy treasures of the church, together with the Lord's supper . . . it was a privilege to be allowed to pray it . . . great reverence and awe surrounded it . . . this awesome reverence before the Lord's Prayer was a reality in the ancient church, which, unfortunately, has been lost to us today for the most part.'[2]

Given the well-known complexities of our natures, with motives, desires and ambitions moving in different directions, it is extremely difficult to know when one is being straightforward with the Lord. Yet, endlessly 'peeling the onion' of introspection is a futile and depressing business. The best we can do (and it is the best) is to hand our lives over to the great kindness of our 'Abba, Father'. 'This then is how we know that we belong to the truth and how we set our hearts at rest in his presence whenever our hearts condemn us. For God is greater than our hearts, and he knows everything' (1 John 3:19,20).

Glory – presence

If the sincerity of our love for the Father is a fundamental issue for us, surely it interests him even more. Could this be one reason why he allows difficult times to come to us, which seem a contradiction of a father's love? How else will he, or we, ever know the quality of our love? I wonder if what I'm pleased to call my 'devotion' to God is little better than cupboard love? Am I in this Christian life in order to keep on the right side of the great Supplier? Or might there be just a trace of Job's superb 'though he slay me, yet will I hope in him' (Job 13:15)? It continues to be a speculative talking point until a crisis appears and my life is shaken to its roots. Then, one way or the other, I soon have the answer to my question. Yet in the matter of giving God the adoration of our hearts, in seeking the renown of his name, his kingdom, and his will, as the origin of all blessings, we may still be undecided. A voice whispers that the Father is well able to take care of his own glory. We may still be uneasy about the apparent mismatch between the loving Almighty Father and the God who insists on top place.

Light dawns once we learn that in Scripture, the root meaning of 'glory' is 'weightiness', weight. The glory of God is the 'heaviness' of his presence, the antithesis of an ephemeral, insubstantial, misty deity. God's glory is the substance of his presence, all that he is, all the grace and love, majesty and wisdom, justice and compassion, faithfulness and holiness, joy and generosity, amounting to a weight of glory. Thus, when God returned to Israel's temple, Ezekiel described the moment in two ways: both 'the glory of the LORD filled the temple', and God saying 'This is where I will live' (Ezekiel 43:5,7). His glory is his presence. What greater good could we ever request for society than for God's glory to be its controlling and shaping force? How significant it is that when Jesus stood on the edge of the abyss, only hours before the cross, with the powers of wickedness poised to destroy him and so dismember the Godhead, he entrusted the outcome of the next three days to the glory of the Father's presence (John 17:1,4,5).

To summarise, the Lord's Prayer seeks first the glory of God before all else. Adoration of the Father is like striking a tuning fork to send a note humming through our world, calling all things to respond in praise and obedience. By placing the Father's glory first, Jesus leads to the centre of things, where the vital decisions are made and the outcomes are decided. It is the place where names and kingdoms struggle for the ascendancy. In that place we will ask for the Father's glory to be revealed (Revelation 8:1–5).

Seeing glory

At this point I must confess to a difficulty when it comes to putting into words the doctrine of the Father's glorious presence. Words like 'glory' and 'presence', in spite of everything we have tried to say about them, are, I find, elusive and abstract ideas, the more so because of their awesomeness. I catch myself trying to picture what it is I'm asking for when I ask for the Father's glorious presence in this or that situation. How, I wonder, does the Father's 'weighty' presence touch, protect, woo and delight – or terrify and overthrow? Is it of necessity (being the Almighty Presence), like a thousand tons of TNT exploding? Apparently not, since many have encountered the Father's presence and lived to tell of it. Perhaps further visualisations are necessary in our prayers, in order to save us from being over-analytical of the language we use as we pray. What are the pictures, the symbols, the images, the metaphors and the parables that are true to the subject yet warm our hearts and cause thought to flow as we pray the doctrine of the Father's glory? We are not trying to dictate how God's powerful presence should be revealed – we are simply getting off the tramlines by wondering and imagining how we might request the Father's glory to come among us.

- Could we understand the 'weightiness' of God's glory (his glorious presence) as a *heavy net*, which he casts over our affairs for a catch (John 21:1–14)? A 'net' which also he throws over our demonic enemies (Ephesians 6:10–13).
- Or perhaps we might picture God's presence at work in our world as an *enchanting song*, which calms the mind, delights the heart, and compels people to follow him. After all, the early church saw Jesus as 'Orpheus' whose music could charm the wild beasts out of the forest (Luke 8:26–29). When praying for the Lord to be glorified in the lives of our unbelieving friends, we are asking him to captivate them with his music. Have you never passed an open window and heard a piece of music or a song which stops you in your tracks, and you know you will have no peace until you discover what it is?
- Similarly, you might pray for particular friends to come under the Lord's sway, like a fascinating drama which snags in the imagination and leaves them asking 'what happened next?' Emily Dickinson described this as 'tell all the truth but tell it slant'. Pray for the 'slanted' power of the Lord's presence.

- Or perhaps we might imagine the Lord's glory to be affecting our situation like a masterful conductor who is able to impose his discipline on a chaotic orchestra and even coax beautiful music from it. I think I could with confidence ask the Lord to make his presence known in such a way.
- Or shall we say that the Lord's glory is the supreme reality – but invisible to us until the illuminating Spirit touches the 'eyes of the heart', like Elisha's bewildered servant who saw only the enemy until the Lord opened his eyes and he 'looked and saw the hills full of horses and chariots of fire' (2 Kings 6:17)?
- In our faith-imagining as we pray, we will be awake to the way God's presence may bypass impressive phenomena (wind, earthquake and fire) as he chooses to reveal himself in a mysterious 'gentle whisper' (1 Kings 19:11,12).
- Shall we also be open to the Father's presence as a 'weight of joy' coming upon people in their need, as at Cana when Jesus first revealed his glory by transforming water into the finest wine (John 2:1–11)?

Our Father in heaven

The political rhetoric about world peace and prosperity is changing very rapidly. Having treated the world as a useful building site for a 'new order' of our making, national leaders are now more cautious and non-committal in their claims and promises. We are learning to live with new uncertainties and new groupings between nations. There is even talk of a 'clash of civilisations', and a particularly merciless form of terrorism is on the loose around the world. Religion is looking distinctly unlovely at the moment.

Christians might be shocked at some of these developments but, surely, not surprised. The law of 'dust and ashes' is at work in the natural world, and man's best efforts are conditioned by that law. If prayer were of the world, the product of men's hearts, it too would be subject to the law of dust and ashes. But Jesus, in his first words, lifts his prayer, our prayer, off the ground and roots it in heaven. Not Buddha-like, in an attempt to escape the 'prison' of the created world, but so as to release the prayer that transcends the limitations of this 'law of dust'. Our prayer is lifted out of the world and into heaven where the Father dwells, in order to reach back and down into the deepest heart of the world.

God exists in heaven, which is his throne (Revelation 5). If we have to use words such as sovereign, boundless, free, omnipotent, eternal, incomprehensible and transcendent, their purpose isn't simply to oppose what is limited, time-bound, transient and comprehensible. All those 'heaven' attributes flow from the infinite goodness of the 'Father in heaven' who has made himself our 'Abba, Father' in Jesus Christ, his Son. All of heaven is actualised in the omnipotent grace and mercy of Jesus. The Lord's Prayer is supremely the prayer of hope and, therefore, it is the prayer our world most desperately needs. Only heaven can give transcendent, enduring and final meaning to our earthly hopes, which, otherwise, are hopelessly confined to the law of dust and ashes.

Questions for reflection and discussion

1. Are you quite convinced that your prayers for your own concerns will fall naturally into place if your first concerns are for the Father's name, his kingdom and his will?
2. Read Galatians 4:6. God 'sent the Spirit of his Son into our hearts, the Spirit who calls out "Abba, Father".' Can you hear the Spirit's voice in your heart? Listen for him, listen to him and then repeat after him 'Abba, Father'.
3. Do you find any of the 'visualisings' of the Lord's glorious (weighty) presence helpful (p 35,36)? Invent three of your own: symbols, images, metaphors, or even parables which help your thought to flow as you 'pray the doctrine of the Father's glory'.

Chapter 4

THE APPRENTICESHIP

A woman enters a room buzzing with playgroup toddlers. One small child looks up as she comes in, laughs and calls out in recognition. Prayer begins here; it is the primary expression of recognition towards our heavenly Father, planted within our hearts by the Holy Spirit (Galatians 4:6). Paul saw the connection between prayer, recognition and joy, 'Be joyful always; pray continually; give thanks in all circumstances, for this is God's will for you in Christ Jesus' (1 Thessalonians 5:16–18). At the start of the day, the Spirit (if we will discern his touch) causes us to look up into the Father's face and smile in recognition.

Prayer is a gift from God; it is a grace, grounded in the child-like assurance that he meets us in his Son, eager to know what is on our heart. Our words matter to him; they 'make his day', just as considerate parents allow their children's needs and aspirations to affect their own agenda for the day. Prayer 'changes' God, in the sense that he acts differently because we have spoken with him.

How should we pray? Experience has convinced most of us that if left to our own devices we are soon using God as we do the ATM cash-dispensing machine in the high street. But he loves his children far too much, and has far more in mind for them, than to allow 'prayer' to slide into such banality. James warned '. . . You do not have, because you do not ask God. When you ask, you do not receive, because you ask with wrong motives, that you may spend what you get on your pleasures' (James 4:2,3). One way of responding to an uncooperative cash machine is to give it a sharp kick in the right spot. Another way would be to read through the instructions carefully again (or for the first time!). Our praying needs guidance and regulation, so that we don't ask blindly, stubbornly and arbitrarily, and then complain that 'prayer doesn't work'. We have Jesus' prayer. By using it wisely, said Calvin, 'we may serve our apprenticeship in true prayer'.[1]

The previous chapter considered how the Lord's Prayer helps us to pray the doctrine of the Godhead, that most profound and far-reaching of all prayers. Of the six petitions, the first three are a statement of the glory of the Father in terms of his name, his kingdom and his will. (Matthew 6:9,10). We are ready now to contemplate each of the three and consider how we might pray them to the Father.

'Hallowed be your name'

God loves truth, light and clarity; he loathes deceit. Therefore he signs his name to everything he makes. Evil detests the light, preferring to go nameless or under various pseudonyms. We speak about 'nameless' fears, nameless evils, nameless miseries, nameless horrors, whose origins are out of sight. Satan is the father of all who write mischievous anonymous letters.

The Lord took an enormous risk in releasing his holy name into this unholy world. At our own modest level we are aware of danger in allowing others to get control of our name and signature, hence the spectacular spread of the document-shredding machine. You will have seen, also, coins which have suffered in circulation, so that the image and inscription are worn, defaced and illegible. God's name suffers such an un-hallowing within the world, most obviously through casual blasphemy, but also by our failure to give him the praise for his works and gifts. Thanksgiving due to God is routinely deflected to science, government, fate, chance or even astrology. Man chooses, George Herbert remarked, to 'rest in nature, not the God of nature'. This is wholesale robbery. God's name, his honour and his glory no more belong to the world as its property than the play belongs to the audience. Thus a gigantic fraud is embedded deep in the heart of a non-worshipping society.

God warns 'You shall not misuse the name of the LORD your God, for the LORD will not hold anyone guiltless who misuses his name' (Exodus 20:7).

God's name is already hallowed before we pray for such a thing. The great signs of his glory are in the world like shining lights: 'Christ has died – Christ is risen – Christ will come again' are the decisive realities which establish and hallow the Father's name over against the principalities and powers of darkness. Our part is to pray that the 'hallowing' which Christ won for the Father is seen and received more deeply and widely by a fundamental shift and transformation in the heart of society: from God-ignoring, God-denying, God-hating, God-rejecting, God-blaspheming, to a place where he is honoured. Just to say such things shows that we are talking of a movement far beyond the capacity of Christians to deliver. Only the Lord can bring about such a fundamental shift, but as Christians we have our part. In practice we cannot do better than to take up and make our own the biblical vision which has always been at the heart of authentic worship.

Pray the psalms

The psalmists loved to detail creation in all its variety, naming and calling on each thing to play its part in glorifying the Lord's name simply by being what it should be, what God intends it to be. A typical example is Psalm 148:

> Praise the LORD.
>
> Praise the LORD from the heavens;
>   praise him in the heights above.
> Praise him, all his angels,
>   praise him, all his heavenly hosts.
> Praise him, sun and moon,
>   praise him, all you shining stars.
> Praise him, you highest heavens
>   and you waters above the skies.

Let them praise the name of the LORD,
　　for he commanded and they were created.
He set them in place for ever and ever –
　　he gave a decree that will never pass away.

Praise the LORD from the earth,
　　you great sea creatures and all ocean depths,
lightning and hail, snow and clouds,
　　stormy winds that do his bidding,
you mountains and all hills,
　　fruit trees and all cedars,
wild animals and all cattle,
　　small creatures and flying birds,
kings of the earth and all nations,
　　you princes and all rulers on earth,
young men and maidens,
　　old men and children.

Let them praise the name of the LORD,
　　for his name alone is exalted;
　　his splendour is above the earth and the heavens.
He has raised up for his people a horn,
　　the praise of all his saints,
　　of Israel, the people close to his heart.

Praise the LORD.

Other sources of praise include Psalms 19, 33, 36 . . . 145, 147, 149 and 150.

The understanding of the world implicit in the psalms, as symbolical and sacramental, reflects Isaiah's immense realisation:

> Holy, holy, holy is the LORD Almighty;
> the whole earth is full of his glory.

Isaiah 6:3

We hallow the Father's name when we honour creation as the theatre of his presence and self-revelation. If so, then it follows that 'everything' has value and deserves closer attention than we usually afford. George Herbert said about our relationship to the created world:

> Only to man thou has made known thy ways,
> put the pen alone in his hand
> And made him secretary of thy praise.[2]

Only human beings have the mystical gift of language, for our go-between role, the priestly work of speaking to God on behalf of the world, and to the world on behalf of God. To do what a good secretary is there to do, see to it that the message is communicated in both directions. In practice it will mean lifting up our world to God in vicarious praise; to pray and praise on behalf of the world, as though the world speaks to God through our mind and life.

There seem to be two ways in which we act as secretary of God's praise. First, we can cultivate the habit of a praising mind as we move through the day. That lovely little tree in the next street, when did anyone last give thanks to God for it? Gerard Manley Hopkins practised this wondering, praising attentiveness:

Pied Beauty

> Glory be to God for dappled things –
> For skies of couple-colour as a brinded cow;
> For rose-moles all in stipple upon trout that swim;
> Fresh-firecoal chestnut-falls; finches' wings;
> Landscape plotted and pieced – fold, fallow and plough;
> And all trades, their gear and tackle and trim.
>
> All things counter, original, spare, strange;
> Whatever is fickle, freckled, (who knows how?)
> With swift, slow; sweet, sour; adazzle, dim;
> He fathers-forth whose beauty is past change:
> Praise him.[3]

Daily life is thus redeemed by a continuing act of 'saying grace' as we fulfil our 'priest-secretary' ministry between heaven and our little bit of earth. An advance of that practice is to look for the *symbolic* aspect in all created things. Thus children are both what they are, beautiful and lively, but they are also a symbol of the kingdom. Everything is both itself and speaks also of something else, higher in God. We hallow his name by these expectant, respectful attitudes, because he has endowed his creation with a symbolism which points to him.

The practice of routine thanks giving throughout the day as practised in Judaism is highly instructive. The serious Jew is expected to give thanks to God one hundred times a day. They have a short form of words, leading into each prayer which goes, 'Holy One of Blessing, your presence fills Creation . . .' followed by thanks for things seen, tasted, felt, heard, enjoyed. The rabbis remark that 'Blessings keep our awareness of life's holy potential ever present. They awaken us to our lives. Every blessing says I am grateful to be a creature and to remind myself and God that life is good. With each blessing uttered we extend the boundaries of the sacred and ritualise our love of life. One hundred times a day, everywhere we turn, everything we touch, everyone we see. The blessing can be whispered. No one even need hear. No one but the Holy One. "Holy One of Blessing, your presence fills the Universe. Your presence fills me." '[4]

The great cry 'Let everything that has breath praise the LORD.' (Psalm 150:6) arises from the conviction that the whole reason for the world's existence is to reveal and hallow God's name. Life in all its everyday humdrum ordinariness is full of potential for praise. A small cat is about as ordinary as anything could be, but consider what that unusual man Christopher Smart saw as he contemplated his cat.

> For I will consider my Cat Jeoffrey.
> For he is the servant of the Living God, duly
> and daily serving him.
> For at the first glance of the glory of God in the East

he worships in his way.
For is this done by wreathing his body seven times
round with elegant quickness.
For then he leaps up to catch the musk, which is the
blessing of God upon his prayer.
For he rolls upon prank to work it in.
For having done duty and received blessing he begins
to consider himself . . .

For the dexterity of his defence is an instance of the
love of God to him exceedingly.
For he is quickest to his mark of any creature.
For he is tenacious of his point.
For he is a mixture of gravity and waggery.
For he knows that God is his Saviour.
For there is nothing sweeter than his peace when at rest.
For there is nothing brisker than his life when in motion.
For he is of the Lord's poor and so indeed is he
called by benevolence perpetually – Poor Jeoffrey!
poor Jeoffrey! the rat has bit thy throat.
For I bless the name of the Lord Jesus that Jeoffrey is better.
For the divine Spirit comes about his body to sustain
it in compleat cat.

Christopher Smart (1722–1771)[5]

'Your kingdom come'

The first petition asked for the hallowing of the name that is already hallowed. The second prays for the coming of the kingdom that has already come. 'Already come', meaning that in Christ everything has been done that needs to be done to establish the kingdom of God in the world. The reign of God is not a spatial, territorial concept but a dynamic concept; it is God's rule in action. The King is the kingdom and it is the ecstatic cry of the New Testament that Christ reigns throughout the totality of creation, seen and unseen, by the 'incomparably great power . . . [which God] exerted in Christ when he raised him from the dead and seated him at his right hand in the heavenly realms, far above all rule and authority, power and dominion, and every title that can be given, not only in the present age but also in the one to come . . .' (Ephesians 1:19–21). To the Philippians, Paul makes a glorious canticle from that truth when he writes that the king went to the cross. 'Therefore God exalted him to the highest place and gave him the name that is above every name, that at the name of Jesus every knee should bow, in heaven and on earth and under the earth, and every tongue confess that Jesus Christ is Lord, to the glory of God the Father' (Philippians 2:9–11). It is done, settled, accomplished, finished. In Christ, the kingdom has come. Otherwise, if in fact he does not reign throughout heaven and earth, 'Christ on the throne' is only a figurehead, a metaphor.

Why, then, are we commanded to pray for the kingdom to come? And if it has come already, why doesn't the world show more convincing evidence of its presence? CEB Cranfield comments 'The Kingdom has both come and is still to come because Jesus has come and is to come again.'[6] Jesus is the key. He is Lord over all, but he is out of sight. Not absent, but hidden. His victory over all the dark powers that threaten creation was total and complete through his incarnation; but it is concealed from the world, a 'veiled manifestation'. He revealed the kingdom, but not in an incontrovertible manner that leaves us with no choice but to assent, like it or not. Therefore, 'Your kingdom come' is not asking for God's reign to expand from little to much, from partial to complete, but from veiled to manifest, from hidden to revealed. The kingdom in its fullness came in Christ, since he came in his fullness. We do not pray for something more complete to come, but for that which is already complete to come out from behind its curtains and be manifested in all its glory. (The book of Revelation suggests what is behind the curtain; see chapters 4 and 5.) 'Your kingdom come.' Our hope does not increase from less to more, since

Christ is, already, all our hope. The kingdom does not follow the curve of an incremental development; it moves from faith to sight.

And how shall we visualise the coming (manifested) kingdom as we pray for it? What does the kingdom look like? *It is the life and purpose of the world in accordance with the intentions of the creator.* It includes the church, but it is far greater than the limits of the church. The King's agenda reads 'All things' in heaven and earth. The church, which knows and confesses these things, is set in society to be a sample of the kingdom, a clue to its life and love, a signpost pointing society towards the King. Thus we pray for our churches to be inspired in their witness to the kingdom, which has come and is still to come when Christ comes again. A witness that both 'shows' and 'tells', for we must not split the good news of the kingdom (Mark 1:14,15), dividing spiritual message from practical service, any more than we would dream of dividing Christ into a spiritual chaplain for our souls and a 'social worker' Christ for our physical requirements. He is one. The kingdom and the good news of the kingdom are one. Our mission must be one, all of which casts us upon the Lord with the urgent prayer, *'Your Kingdom come, Lord, in your time and your way. But take us, and our busy programmes, our preaching, teaching and witnessing, our service to others, into your purposes. Above all things, fill our hearts with joy and great confidence as we look for you coming among us.'*

'Your will be done'

Why did Martin Luther refer to this third petition as a 'fearful prayer'? Nothing could be less fearful or more desirable than the prospect of heaven's garden city here on earth: the love, the peace, the joy, and a light to outshine the sun (Revelation 21), conditions symbolised by swords-into-ploughshares, and small children playing happily and safely around the cobra's nest (Isaiah 2:2–5; 11:8). This is a beguiling picture of God's will for the world, a hope that gives ultimate meaning to all our hopes in this life. It hardly needs saying that God's will should be done on earth as in heaven, now, in the sense that this world ought to be a far more pleasant place than it is for vast numbers of the human family. My guess is that Luther thought the prayer 'fearful' for another reason.

The will of God 'on earth as in heaven' is a radiant prospect and a joy to pray. Complications appear with the realisation that the will of God for the world – vast, rolling on, immeasurable – includes his personal will for my life! His general will for the cosmos is tied up with the person of Jesus and the universal requirement that 'at the name of Jesus every knee should bow . . . and every tongue confess that Jesus Christ is Lord' (Philippians 2:10,11). The general will of God is thrilling, but his particular will threatens my own will, which is a 'fearful' prospect. For God's will to be 'done on earth as in heaven' requires the surrender of our self-will, and what was an easy prayer for the world out there, suddenly becomes a request that the Lord Jesus become my personal Lord, and his will become the first concern of my will. In fact this prayer isn't possible until one has surrendered to the authority of the Lord. 'Fearful', for who knows where it will lead or what it will involve. Yet in one sense we do know. When the Father's will is 'done on earth (on our little bit of the earth) as it is in heaven' we become agents of his vast purposes and participants in the processes of the Holy Spirit, whereby the God who says 'I am making everything new' (Revelation 21:5) is fulfilling his designs among us here and now. Our lives, when delivered from the stifling confinement to self-will, and into the freedom of the will of God, take on extraordinary significance.

So, how shall we pray this prayer? Ask for the grace to know, love and embrace the will of God. Have Romans 12:1,2 open in front of you and allow it to inform and guide prayer for yourself, for Christians you know, and for congregations, pastors, leaders, teachers and those who are arguing Christ's case in the media and other places of influence.

Paul writes:

> Therefore, I urge you, brothers and sisters, in view of God's mercy, to offer your bodies as living sacrifices, holy and pleasing to God . . . Do not conform any longer to the pattern of this world, but be transformed by the renewing of your mind. Then you will be able to test and approve what God's will is – his good, pleasing and perfect will.
>
> Romans 12:1,2

Questions for reflection and discussion

1. Calvin suggested that by using the Lord's Prayer wisely 'we may serve our apprenticeship in true prayer' (p 39). An 'apprenticeship' implies a grounding in sound principles. Compare the usual structure, and the order of priorities, in your own prayer with what Jesus gives in his prayer.
2. 'That lovely little tree in the next street, when did anyone last give thanks to God for it?' (p 42).
   Make a conscious effort, today, to act as 'secretary to God's praise'. Is Christopher Smart doing that, or is he just being silly about Jeoffrey his cat? (p 43,44).
3. How, in practice, do you cope with the routine misuse of the Lord's name in everyday life? (p 39). Do the rabbis point the way by 'blessing' (thanking) God for everything because 'Blessings keep our awareness of life's holy potential ever present' (p 43)?
4. The Church is in the world to 'show and tell' the kingdom of God (p 46). How faithful is your own congregation to that calling?

Chapter 5

WITH EMPTY HANDS

'Give us today our daily bread'

There is such a thing as godly materialism, as well as the godless sort. 'Flesh' is the most material word in the language, and the Son of God 'became flesh' (John 1:14). People of 'flesh' need to eat. While acknowledging that bread is also a symbol of the Bread of Life, we will avoid any hyper-spiritualising tendencies impatient with basic, this-world, concerns for bread on the table. After all, when Jesus instructed his disciples to 'go into your room, close the door and pray to your Father' (Matthew 6:6) he most probably meant the larder, which was the only room capable of being shut, in most Israelite houses. It would be difficult to ignore the demands of the stomach in an atmosphere heavy with the aromas of cinnamon and other spices, or, for the poor man at prayer, the empty shelves surrounding him.

When Jesus 'became flesh' the Almighty Father crossed the line to become personally concerned with everything we think of under the term 'daily bread': clothes, shelter, work and health care, all of which are threatened with the possibility of anxiety, causing problems to life as described in Isaiah's vision of God's will for the human family:

> Never again will there be in it
>   infants who live but a few days,
>   or older people who do not live out their years;
> those who die at a hundred
>   will be thought mere youths;

> those who fail to reach a hundred
> > will be considered accursed.
> They will build houses and dwell in them;
> > they will plant vineyards and eat their fruit.
> No longer will they build houses and others live in them,
> > or plant and others eat.
> For as the days of a tree,
> > so will be the days of my people;
> my chosen ones will long enjoy
> > the works of their hands.

Isaiah 65:20–22

Today churches around the world are using the Isaiah vision (or Isaiah agenda) as a strategy for their mission, with its clear objectives[1]

- that children do not die,
- that old people live in dignity,
- that those who build houses live in them, and
- that those who build vineyards eat their fruit.

It is evangelistic because its strategy aims at ways to awaken, or reawaken, personal faith in Jesus Christ and to proclaim the character of God. What is God like? Isaiah's vision reveals a compassionate Father who is on the side of the vulnerable, the weak and the defenceless. 'A father to the fatherless, a defender of widows, is God in his holy dwelling. God sets the lonely in families . . .' (Psalm 68:5,6). Not content with his knowledge of us as our Creator, in Jesus Christ he became one of us, exposed to the full gamut of dangers, anxieties and joys that make up our lives. What is he like? Try him with the prayer, 'Father in heaven, give us today our daily bread.' By taking up our urgent, practical requirements he changes what is a cause for fear and anxiety into an opportunity to trust and prove him. He wouldn't place his reputation on the line by urging us to trust him for bread if he hadn't enough already in his storehouses. All over the world people offer up this prayer for their daily bread – which amounts to a vast order! Yet the Father has never thought it necessary to edit the prayer out of Scripture.

But what are we to make of mass starvation in parts of Africa and those appalling pictures of shattered parents and skeletal children?

I'm no economist, but even I can understand that there is enough food in the world but that abundance and plenty become scarcity and hunger because of our insatiable greed and fear. Thus the rich countries are plagued with obesity while poor peoples suffer malnutrition. Because enough is never enough, or never cheap enough, for the rich, others elsewhere go hungry and sick. All too often, situations of famine and starvation are bound up with war and corruption. Ruthless warlords, profiteering merchants and corrupt politicians between them filter out desperately needed aid. In that startling cartoon portrayal of the processes of starvation and death in the book of Revelation, four horsemen ride across the earth (Revelation 6). We have little trouble identifying them, since they regularly fill our TV screens. The rider on the white horse is conquest (v 2); followed, inevitably, by the rider on the red horse representing rebellion (v 4); followed, inevitably, by the black horse, for famine (vs 5,6); followed, again inevitably, by the rider on the pale horse, which is Death (v 8). They travel together and operate in sequence.

Also it is apparent even to this non-economist that, because human sin is behind the continuing scandal of poverty in a richly endowed world, we must humbly return to the Lord, confessing our mercilessness and learning from him how we ought to relate to the human family:

• Scripture teaches that Adam never owned the garden but worked in it as the estate manager for the good of creation and to the glory of God; we must renounce materialism's funda-mental lie that we *own* our lives, ourselves and our stuff. We are entrusted with it as trustees or tenants, and will soon have to give account to the Lord of our stewardship.

- Secondly, whenever we sincerely pray, 'Give us today our daily bread', we are inviting God's personal intervention in the production, regulation, distribution, and use of our food (which is not ours!). Our text will be: 'The earth is the LORD's, and everything in it, the world, and all who live in it' (Psalm 24:1).

- Next, we need to recover, or discover for the first time, a proper sense of our economic dependence on God, which is a very elusive attitude to acquire. We are obviously dependent on our jobs as the primary means of getting our daily bread. In that sense who isn't a 'wage slave'? But the employer is in God's hands, just as the creative processes of nature are in his gift also. In Austin Farrer's phrase 'God makes the world make itself' as nature fulfils its tasks on many levels: atomic, molecular, cellular, vegetable, animal, social, each plane interacting to 'make the world'. Christ is the informing, guiding, shaping wisdom behind the nature that supplies our food (Colossians 1:15–17; Hebrews 1:2,3).

- If we are serious when we ask the Father to 'give us our daily bread' it follows we will receive our food with gratitude and thanksgiving. Gratitude works a wonderful chemistry in the soul: thankful people simply cannot become gluttons. They are more likely to have something left over for others. If we practice the truth that 'everything is gift', we too will be swept along by the dynamic of generosity. Thankful people are givers.

- Finally, our daily bread, however routine it may seem, is a sign of the Father's providential love and care at every level:

> You prepare a table before me
>   in the presence of my enemies.
> You anoint my head with oil;
>   my cup overflows.
>
> Psalm 23:5

'Forgive us our debts'

Many would rather the prayer concluded with the previous petition. If the Father supplies our daily bread, surely that's all we
need; now we can get on with leading our lives as we think best.
They feel that talk of 'debt, temptation and the evil one', over-
complicates things unnecessarily. That is a superficial diagnosis
of our condition, typical of the prevailing materialistic interpretation of life which states human 'need' chiefly in terms of what
is lacking or defective: insufficient or defective hospitals, schools,
housing, employment opportunity, pensions and so on. If only
we, or 'they', could improve essential services, so the argument
runs, contentment will appear as sure as day follows night.

The three remaining petitions are, therefore, a head-on challenge to materialism. Jesus said to Satan, 'People do not live on
bread alone, but on every word that comes from the mouth of
God' (Matthew 4:4). 'Yes' to bread, but emphatically 'No' to
bread *alone*, or money *alone*, power *alone*, sex *alone* as the moti-
vation and dynamic for a person's life. Our problem is essentially not one of *defective* goods, but *defection* from God. We are
rebellious, alienated and adrift from God (but not God from
us). We are 'debtors' to God. He is our Creator, Provider and
Father, and we owe him the adoration of our hearts. Unwilling,
and unable to pay, we continue to default, offending and
exploiting the Father's long-suffering love. The debt piles up as
we routinely fail to meet our obligation to give him first place
over all else. We are debtors to God.

However plentiful and nutritious our 'daily bread', we merely
continue to be well-fed debtors. Unable to reach down into our
deepest selves where the debt accumulates, the sin of our indebtedness stains everything it touches – and if the debt continues to
accumulate, day in and day out, as we perversely withhold the
praise of our lives due to God, then our situation resembles a
farmyard where a deranged farmer feeds, waters and pampers the
pigs but never cleans out their sty, as it rots away in the rising levels
of muck and mire. An absurd picture, and yet there are people who

never attempt spiritual mucking-out. For years, decades, or perhaps an entire lifetime they continue without seeking forgiveness for their sin, or cleansing from its defilement.

The prayer teaches that the Father hasn't waited until his debt-ridden children get around to asking him for help. Christ has lived our life, honoured the Father in our place, and paid our debt completely and finally on the cross. It is done.

We know that he will forgive us our debt, since the debt has been covered in Christ. The Lord's Prayer is wide enough to embrace all of us, because it goes deep enough to reach and heal our indebtedness.

Father in heaven, in the person of your Son you have put yourself in our place so that our disordered lives might be healed. In Christ, you have washed away our sin and cancelled all our debts. Jesus has obeyed and suffered in our place, and now we are released, guilt-free and debt-free, into the life and mission of your kingdom. You command us to take our eyes off the past and to look ahead and, in the power and love of the Holy Spirit, gladly offer to you the adoration of our lives in everything, everyday. Amen.

'As we also have forgiven our debtors'

Is this a price we pay in order to receive the Father's forgiveness? No, it is a criterion by which we prove to ourselves that we have understood God's forgiveness. If we respond to our outstanding debts, not by hopelessly trying to pay them off, but by handing ourselves over to the mercy of God, we cannot but forgive any who have offended against him. It is as if we are saying 'Father please forgive me my sin. Indeed I know that in Christ your Son you already have forgiven me. Father, I think I am beginning to understand a little of the wonder and mystery of your unconditional forgiveness because I find myself treating other people with mercy. What you have done for me is being reflected in my attitudes to others.'

The joy and hope of sins forgiven and cancelled will surely enlarge our heart toward others. This is, in fact, no big deal! God is not asking of us a great moral effort, an angelic exertion of virtue in showing forgiveness and mercy to others. No great fuss, no hounding people with our 'forgiveness!' It should come quite naturally because, by the grace of God, that's the sort of person we are becoming. George Herbert warned, 'He that cannot forgive others breaks the bridge over which he must pass himself; for every man has need to be forgiven.'[2] The first and decisive piece of information about Christians is that they are forgiven in Christ, their debts to God paid for.

If, on the other hand, you find that in certain circumstances, involving particular people, you cannot forgive, doesn't that place a question mark against the forgiveness you have received from the Father? Jesus assumed that the divine forgiveness we have received makes us able to forgive. Prove the sincerity of your prayer by extending forgiveness to others. Forgiveness that does not forgive is not forgiveness.

Clearly the claims that 'we also have forgiven our debtors' give a taste of the grace and hope of the gospel. It is a tangy, intriguing, delicious taste, where we have forgiven freely without reservation, wholeheartedly. Pray for your congregation to be a 'community of forgiveness'. But we have to ask why in fact society doesn't see or hear that message more clearly. Luther said that 'accusing is the true business of the Devil', who uses two ways of smothering forgiveness before it can do its gracious work. First he piles on the sense of guilt so that a Christian goes through life with the shadow of failure across his mind. Satan points out the person's sin to such an extent that the sense of the Father's forgiveness is obscured, like fog screening out the sun. This happens when Satan persuades us to look more into ourselves than into the Father's face. Self-analysis and self-recrimination feed off each other until despair, depression and perhaps unbelief replace the exuberant sense of sins and debts forgiven. In that state of mind forgiveness seems too good to be true; and our acceptance of forgiveness seems like we are letting ourselves off the hook too easily. The result is Christian misery.

Satan's second trick is, if anything, even subtler, with disastrous effects on the church. He persuades Christians to concentrate less on forgiveness and more on society's morality. We become moralisers, pointing out shortcomings and failure, quick to seize on faults, and all in the name of 'upholding Christian standards in society'. But the Father's forgiven people are in the business of forgiveness. 'As we also have forgiven our debtors' indicates that we are the light of the world, and the salt of the earth, in a society which needs the salt and light of generous, open-hearted, real forgiveness. Doesn't it strike you how sour, resentful and unforgiving the national mood has become? I almost flinch from going into our local newsagent with its display of headlines that are invariably mean, spiteful, delighting in failure, without a shred of generosity or forgiveness in them. Individuals are lampooned, campaigns of derision are pursued against politicians or other prominent people, ethnic groups are blamed for our national shortcomings, and the worst possible slant is placed on quite unremarkable items. Different social groups are held up for ridicule, or as a source of envy. The muck and the mire in the pigsty of the national psyche accumulate, infection spreads, we become sick.

Against those miserable tendencies, Christ's people are called to speak and act a message of astounding forgiveness. The doors of the church, like the doors of our prayers, stand wide open to welcome all comers to the Father's banquet of forgiveness and reconciliation.

Questions for reflection and discussion

1. Look again at the background to Jesus' concern for our 'daily bread', as expressed in the Isaiah vision. This is our God. This is the God we invite others to know and to follow as his co-workers in the Isaiah agenda. What are you doing to portray the heart of God through concern for the vulnerable, children and old people? How involved are you and your congregation in the work of the agenda?

2. What do you expect to happen when you pray 'Father, forgive us our debts'? Consider one Christian's insights: 'When God forgives, he does not simply pronounce or simply record a sentence; when God forgives, the well-spring of life turns from bitter to sweet, the acid of sin ceases to corrode, and living waters irrigate the soul, we stop shrivelling, we begin to grow.'[3] Could it be that 'forgiveness' remains the fundamental need of our churches, and of our individual lives?

Chapter 6

AGAINST THE DARKNESS

'And lead us not into temptation, but deliver us from the evil one.'

With the petitions for our daily bread and the forgiveness of our sins, we might expect the Lord's Prayer to come quietly to rest, our physical and spiritual requirements covered. Instead, Jesus suddenly raises it to crisis point in the shape of the 'evil one's' hostility to all who seek the Father's glory. Everything previously prayed for will stand or fall on the outcome of this final request. The matter of our 'debts', amassed because of our refusal to honour the Father in our lives, has exposed our spiritual bankruptcy and the fact that we are easy prey to the Great Tempter as he plots our demise at every turn.

So serious is our situation as Christians in this world that the best thing we can do is to throw ourselves onto the grace of God with the desperate cry 'deliver us . . .!' Thus the Lord's Prayer, which we customarily use as a well-worn mantra, recited rather than thought about, loved for the sense of calm it conveys, dramatically peaks with a stark statement of unseen warfare against the powers of darkness, and a call to arms.

What sort of world?

In the same breath Jesus spoke of our daily bread and of 'the evil one', the commonplace and the unimaginable, the visible and the invisible, in a way that bewilders the secular mind. How did Jesus see the world? He placed this-world life of people and things against the background of cosmic spiritual conflict. Without the biblical revelation, we will misunderstand the nature of the forces at work, both for and against us. Thus as we follow Jesus at work in the Gospels we see him responding to sin, need and suffering by slipping under the appearance of things to grapple with forces at work behind them. The supreme physician, he treated the *cause* of people's disorders, not their *symptoms*. He is creation's Redeemer, because he overcame creation's great disruptor, the devil.

Jesus' exorcisms are reported in the Gospels as battles against evil powers (eg Mark 1:23–28). He describes his invasion into the domain of evil in human society as 'no-one can enter a strong man's house and carry off his possessions without first tying up the strong man. Then his house can be plundered' (Mark 3:27). His victories over demonic power are not random, isolated incursions into the satanic realm. Rather they send out signals that the Saviour of the world is here, and it is the beginning of the end for the evil one. Why Jesus attributes such importance to the authority over the spirits exercised by his disciples is to be seen from the cry of joy which greets the report of the disciples on their return, that the spirits had to yield to their commands: 'Lord, even the demons submit to us in your name!' He replied, 'I saw Satan fall like lightning from heaven' (Luke 10:17,18). The casting of Satan out of the heavenly world presupposes an earlier battle in heaven like that described in Revelation 12:7–9. Jesus' visionary cry of joy leaps over the interval of time before the final crises and sees in the exorcisms performed by the disciples the dawn of the annihilation of Satan. This stage had already been reached: the evil spirits are powerless, Satan is being destroyed (Luke 10:18), paradise is opening up (v 19), and the names of the redeemed are written in heaven (v 20). All this is visible only to the believer. Satan still exercises his power, but where people believe Jesus, the cry of joy rings out that permeates the whole of the New Testament: 'the power of Satan has been broken!'[1] Only a Christian mind, illuminated by the biblical revelation of Christ and his work, will grasp what is going on in the struggle between good and evil, joy and misery. It is this vision that illuminates prayer with joy and hope.

A God-shaping

The idea that our Father would ever 'lead us into temptation' sounds strange and disturbing. Is Jesus actually suggesting that we need to plead with the Father to do us no harm? Our anxieties are mitigated by the realisation that 'temptation' in the New Testament carries also the meaning of 'testing'; another translation gives 'and do not put us to the test' (REB). At the same time, New Testament writers embrace 'tests, trials, sufferings, temptations' as necessary for our progress to maturity. Grown-up Christians know the value of testings. James writes:

> Consider it pure joy, my brothers and sisters, whenever you face trials of many kinds, because you know that the testing of your faith develops perseverance. Perseverance must finish its work so that you may be mature and complete, not lacking anything. . . . Blessed are those who persevere under trial, because when they have stood the test, they will receive the crown of life that God has promised to those who love him.
>
> James:1:2–4,12

Paul is, if anything, even more enthusiastic about the benefits of testings:

> . . . We rejoice in the hope of the glory of God. Not only so, but we also rejoice in our sufferings, because we know that suffering produces perseverance; perseverance, character; and character, hope. And hope does not disappoint us, because God has poured out his love into our hearts by the Holy Spirit, whom he has given us.
>
> Romans 5:2–5

What precisely the 'testings, trials, temptations, sufferings' experienced by the New Testament church were we are not told; no doubt the details were withheld so that Christians in each future generation are then free to read into the text their own testings – whatever 'tests' our faith in the Lord or 'tempts' us to give up for the sake of an easier life. Essential to our soul-making, they act like the fire in a forge in which hard or brittle metal is made malleable and workable. Trials and temptations in the shaping hands of the Spirit act as his skilful hammer blows, 'persuading' the Christian's character into the design God imagines for each. The outcome is a unique, handcrafted one-off piece of work, never to be replicated, bearing all the marks of a God-shaping. Whatever else you ask for in your prayers for other Christians, pray for the grace to 'rejoice in your sufferings'. And remember those who are frankly bewildered by the fact that their heavenly Father would ever allow difficult times to occur for them. Perhaps they assume that the surest sign of his love is a trouble-free life in which success, guidance and blessing arrive on the dot because 'isn't that what a father desires for his children?' In fact what our Father desires is real men and women; thus he takes up and uses all the character-forming materials which happen to be lying about, the knocks and shocks, pitfalls and setbacks which life throws up.

Which is the more grown-up, more glorifying to the Lord, and probably more interesting in the eyes of the world? Is it the Christian who claims (I was in a car when the driver announced this!) 'My heavenly Father always finds me just the right parking place when I drive into town' or the one who takes his chances in the daily mayhem of traffic congestion, like the rest of the human race, transcending petty inconveniences with the cheerful, optimistic dignity of a child of God? Our culture of ease and convenience, efficiency and productivity makes 'testings' seem an intolerable nuisance. An American Christian writes, 'In America, Christians pray for the burden of suffering to be lifted from their back. In the rest of the world, Christians pray for stronger backs so they can bear their suffering. It's why we look away from the bag lady on the street to the displays in the store windows. Why we prefer going to the movies instead of hospitals and nursing homes.' That seems a rather severe criticism, but surely he is correct in suggesting that Christians who expect affluence and comfort as their normal entitlement (their 'human rights'!) will regard afflictions as a sign of failure, or an absent God.

George MacDonald knew poverty, unemployment, near starvation and lung disease, yet he was reported to be 'a sunny, playful man, deeply appreciative of all really beautiful and delicious things that money can buy, and no less deeply content to do without them.' He interpreted his troubles thus, 'Afflictions are but the shadow of God's wings.' When we pray for 'affliction' to be lifted or removed, we have to allow for the possibility that the Lord may need to keep them in our lives a while longer; they exert the essential heat for further shaping. Preachers, Bible teachers, pastors, youth leaders stand in great need of our prayers that they might be wise and courageous enough to dare to teach the biblical interpretation of trials and sufferings in the face of a culture of soft self-pleasing.

So far we have thought of testings as being those events which are part and parcel of being alive in this risky world: in secular language, 'the slings and arrows of outrageous fortune', which can hurt and put a Christian's faith under stress. The Great Enemy knows how to exploit such times: witness how cleverly he exploited Adam's sense of grievance at being denied the fruit of the tree. We can expect trouble from three groups of enemies coming at us from three directions.

The enemy from within

This is the enemy which is ourselves: not God or Satan or anyone else, but ourselves. 'When tempted, no-one should say "God is tempting me." For God cannot be tempted by evil, nor does he tempt anyone; but each of you is tempted when, by your own evil desire, you are dragged away and enticed. Then, after desire has conceived, it gives birth to sin; and sin, when it is full-grown, gives birth to death' (James 1:13–15).

Forgiven, saved people must be realistic about the survival within themselves of 'their own evil desires'; and this is bad news for the blame culture, since the culprit lies within ourselves. Self-love resents and resists all attempts to teach it new ways, so how shall we pray for one another as we struggle with our own 'evil desires'? The classic answer to that question says something about 'the expulsive power of a new affection', meaning that there is limited value in lecturing people on their addiction to something or some practice, if they are 'in love' with it. What must happen is for that old love to be displaced ('expelled') by an incoming new love. A smoker may love his cigarettes so much that he is quite unable to break the habit. Health warnings, lectures, appeals are all ineffectual. Then he falls in love with a woman who tells him how much she hates the smell and taste of tobacco, and suddenly change is possible.

Holy Father, even as I praise you for the gift of new life in Jesus, and for the presence of the sanctifying Holy Spirit, I confess the powerful pull of my own 'evil desires'. You tell me in your word '. . . you have taken off your old self with its practices and have put on the new self, which is being renewed in knowledge in the image of its Creator' (Colossians 3:9,10). Father, your word is truth. Pour into my heart such love for you and for your dear Son that I will grow to hate everything that grieves you. May the power of the new self transform my old 'evil desires' into desires for holiness.

The enemy from the 'atmosphere'

We touched on this aspect of temptation in the first chapter under the heading 'You become what you breathe' (p 10,11). Each culture generates its own characteristic 'atmosphere' or spiritual environment, which its people contribute towards and draw from. Our own is not unfairly described as characterised by 'secular scepticism'; anti-supernatural, anti-revelation, materialistic: its basic confession of faith is 'we are what we have'. In an amusing piece on her passion for shopping at Argos, Kate Muir writes, 'I was there again last week, on another errand in the hellish glare of the store, its Soviet-shortage emptiness belied by the fullness of its catalogue. It contains 13,000 articles.

. . . As I watched the concentration on the faces of those contemplating the laminated catalogue before annotating their purchase slips, I had a fresh inspiration. The shoppers reminded me of monks standing at lecterns in a mediaeval library, reading an illuminated Bible, glossing in the margins.'[2] Argos isn't the danger; things of themselves are not a threat; but faith in the phantom ability of possessions to satisfy, and the almost religious power and function of consumerism feeds into the atmosphere in which we all live and move and have our being.

One intriguing instance of what the spirit of secular scepticism can do to a person's mind is provided by temple dancers in Bali. Schooled from earliest years to enter the trance in which they make their symbolic movements and gestures, the dancers completely lose that ability after even a short exposure to Western attitudes. It is an atmosphere that is able to invade and possess the mind, like a seduction. Is this how we should understand Paul's words that the evil one is 'the ruler of the kingdom of the air' (Ephesians 2:1,2)?

Dear Father, may your Holy Spirit, with the power and illumination of your holy word, so possess my mind and imagination that I will be strong to resist the approach and seductions of godless attitudes and ambitions. Continue with your gracious 'renewing of my mind' (Romans 12:1,2) so that I will be able to discern and choose your will every time.

The enemy from below

Our sins forgiven, reconciled to the Father, now like any healthy child we would like to go outside to play. Yes, certainly, only be aware of dangers out there. Peter describes them vividly:

> Be self-controlled and alert. Your enemy the devil prowls around like a roaring lion looking for someone to devour. Resist him, standing firm in the faith, because you know that your brothers and sisters throughout the world are undergoing the same kind of sufferings.
>
> 1 Peter 5:8,9

In another, even more violent, image (Revelation 12:9) the devil is a multi-headed 'enormous red dragon' that has received a mortal blow in its struggle with Christ:

> The great dragon was hurled down – that ancient serpent called the devil, or Satan, who leads the whole world astray. He was hurled to the earth, and his angels with him.
>
> Revelation 12:9

Time is running out for the creature who, 'filled with fury, because he knows that his time is short' (v 12), concentrates its energies on pursuing and attacking Christ's people in the world.

Notice also the political dimension of satanic strategy; as 'the beast out of the sea' (Revelation 13:1–10), he incarnates himself in the Roman Imperial power coming to Asia Minor from across the Mediterranean; and then again as 'the beast out of the earth' which is the local puppet government under Roman authority (vs 11–18).

Nowhere are anti-Christian regimes described with more power than in Revelation 13: '. . . The whole world was astonished and followed the beast. People worshipped the dragon because he had given authority to the beast, and they also worshipped the beast and asked, "Who is like the beast? Who can make war against him?" ' (vs 3,4).

We speak of this enemy coming to attack us 'from below', signifying the usual direction of the satanic realm (speaking symbolically!). He comes from out of 'the Abyss' (Revelation 9:1–6), the spawning ground of the manifold principalities and powers which enfold the one satanic power. From the Abyss, satanic operatives appear like swarms of locusts, which sting like scorpions but, most significantly, 'their faces resembled human faces' (Revelation 9:7) – hybrids from hell.

Satan is ferocious in his hatred of God's image in creation, but also subtle: 'Satan himself masquerades as an angel of light', wrote Paul in the context of failing church leaders (2 Corinthians 11:13,14). His cunning stratagem is to make himself

65

seem incredible to secularised man, a joke to be binned along with the rest of the occult hocus-pocus. But how anyone could survey the extent and ingenuity of wickedness in the world and still not believe in a Satan is itself incredible to the orthodox Christian mind. As Chesterton put it regarding the behaviour of human beings: 'If it is not true that a divine being fell, then we can only say that one of the animals went entirely off its head.' Jesus took Satan with total seriousness, to the extent that his entire mission could be described as 'The reason the Son of God appeared was to destroy the devil's work' (1 John 3:8). He commanded his disciples to 'watch and pray so that you will not fall into temptation' (Matthew 26:41).

How shall we pray against the satanic enemy from below? Ask God for an attuned sensitivity to the approach of temptation, which we might call the 'Bridget defence'. Bridget of Sweden found that the presence of evil gave her a bitter taste in her mouth. We will more modestly ask the Holy Spirit for powers of discernment and intuition of demonic approach, an early warning faculty to prevent us from stumbling, half asleep into spiritual danger. Why else do we spend time each day, particularly first thing in the morning, in reading Scripture and prayer if not to resensitise our minds to discern the will of God, and unmask the devil in his approaches? Pray for the gift of discerning the spirits, 'test the spirits' (1 John 4:1), and, if you realise that the Lord has given you the gift of wise discernment in these matters, be ready to use it not only for yourself but for others also. We need the discernment of other Christians when we ourselves cannot see what is happening to us.

Secondly, for our defence we invoke the name of Christ which he has set upon his people: 'In my name they will drive out demons' (Mark 16:17). The saving, protecting power of the Name is fundamental to effective Christian witness within current spiritual hostilities. Christ's Name is the hieroglyph for everything he is and achieved when he routed Satan at the cross and the resurrection. Daily we will 'put on' the grace and power of the Name. The book of Revelation goes one better when it speaks of the Lord's Name as his 'seal' on the foreheads of his people (Revelation 9:4; 14:1; 22:4), covering the mind where the decisions are made. Against the torrent of beguiling and persuasive false ideas and images which are daily pumped into the atmosphere and manipulated by the 'enemy from below', only prayer in Christ's Name will guard the mind and keep us faithful and resourceful in truth.

The hyper-testing

Testings, trials, afflictions are all part of the way God governs the world. Jesus instructs us to pray against another level of testing which, if unchecked, will be a testing to destruction. The psalmist may have been confident enough to ask God to 'test me' (Psalm 139:23), but Jesus tasted the full power of demonic testing when alone with Satan in the wilderness (Luke 4:1–13). He directs us to pray for deliverance from that test, which would prove too much for us. *Not* to pray to be spared that extreme examination implies a foolish complacency on our part, a false self-confidence belied by the reality of our weakness. As if in direct reply to our prayer for deliverance from hyper-testing, Paul writes:

> So, if you think you are standing firm, be careful that you don't fall! No temptation has seized you except what is common among people. And God is faithful; he will not let you be tempted beyond what you can bear. But when you are tempted, he will also provide a way out so that you can stand up under it.
>
> 1 Corinthians 10:12,13

Heavenly Father, I won't ask to be spared all testings and difficulties because in your hands they can become a means of blessing, a way of drawing us closer to yourself. But you know our limits! Thank you that Jesus has taken his own experience of temptations back into your presence at the Throne of Grace. I pray for all who at this moment are feeling the pull and heat of temptation, reeling under

67

satanic attack. Keep them under the mighty power of your great Name! For all your children today, 'Lead us not into temptation, but deliver us from the evil one.'

Questions for reflection and discussion

1. Compare the way Jesus saw the world (p 58,59) with the way the atheistic secularism of our culture sees it. With pencil and paper try to represent both world views in diagrams: ie what is the centre, driving force, purpose and direction of each?
2. How is 'evil' understood in both world views? How do you recognise the sovereign power of God in world affairs?
3. Reflect on your own experiences of 'testings, trials, temptations, sufferings' (p 60). Do you agree with the statement that they are 'essential to our soul-making'? What do you make of George MacDonald's observation (derived from his personal experience) that 'Afflictions are but the shadow of God's wings (p 62)?'
4. Spend some time praying in Christ's name against the three directions of demonic attack:

   - the enemy from within (p 62);
   - the enemy from the 'atmosphere' (p 63);
   - the enemy from below (p 64).

Chapter 7

PRAYING CHRIST'S WAY

Eight hundred parents camped all night outside a Stockport school in order to enrol their children next morning on a first-come first-served basis. Parents will go to extraordinary lengths to give their child the best possible start. Do we imagine that God was any less concerned for his Son? He placed Jesus among a people of prayer, for his young life to be formed in their biblical and liturgical traditions. Jesus' remarkable use of the child as a parable of the kingdom suggests rich memories of his own first years. On the inside page of my Bible I have copied Austin Farrer's comment on the unique value of that tradition: 'I read the Old Testament because it is the scriptural inheritance Christ received, it is what he filled his mind with, it is the soil in which his thought grew, it is the alphabet in which he spelled, it is the body of doctrine which he took over and fulfilled.'[1] It also supplied the discipline and the pattern for daily prayer which he took with him through the rest of his life. The Father entrusted the formation of his Son to the wisdom of that tradition, which suggests that before we rush into our own patterns of prayer we should at least pause and consider his.

How different it was in Israel's surrounding world where, by all accounts, serious prayer (to whatever deity) was in a poor way. In the Greek-speaking world, 'philosophy becomes the grave digger of prayer.' The sheer mass of deities and occult practices spawned by the mystery religions and oriental cults stoked the spiritual confusion until the ordinary citizens hardly knew what or who to trust. When Paul arrived in Athens and saw that 'the city was full of idols' (Acts 17:16) he came upon the shrine that exposed Athenian insecurities, an altar to an unknown god (v 23). He took that inscription for his text in his brilliant evangelism. Outside Israel, prayer had declined into superstition and magic; people moved from attitudes of respect towards a more 'consumerist' model of religion, manipulating their 'gods' into giving what was required.

'The three hours of prayer'

Luke comments that on the Sabbath Jesus 'went into the synagogue, as was his custom' (Luke 4:16). We can reasonably assume that he also observed the universally established custom in Judaism of prayer three times a day: at sunrise, mid-afternoon and sunset. The pattern is traced back to Israel's Babylonian captivity and the moment of Daniel's refusal to assimilate to Babylonian idolatry. In defiance of King Darius' edict forbidding prayer to any deity except himself, Daniel 'went home to his upstairs room where the windows opened towards Jerusalem. Three times a day he got down on his knees and prayed, giving thanks to his God, just as he had done before' (Daniel 6:10). A commitment to prayer, which won for Daniel both an encounter with lions and a deliverance by the angel of God who 'shut the mouths of the lions' (v 22), passed into the Jewish spiritual heritage as the 'three hours of prayer', a rhythm of personal and corporate devotion. The prayer itself is called the Tephilla, consisting of a string of psalm-like benedictions.

Specific references in the Gospels to the hour at which Jesus prayed are evidence of his adherence to the three-times-a-day rhythm. We read of him at prayer 'very early in the morning, while it was still dark' (Mark 1:35). Immediately following the feeding of the five thousand, Jesus 'went up on a mountainside to pray' (Mark 6:46). Before choosing the twelve apostles he extended his usual evening prayer time through the night until dawn (Luke 6:12,13). It is also clear that while Jesus used the basic customary pattern of daily prayer he would not allow himself to be limited by it. '. . . Crowds of people came to hear him and to be healed of their sicknesses. But Jesus often withdrew to lonely places and prayed' (Luke 5:15,16 and see 9:18,28). Most significant is the report that at his baptism, '. . . as he was praying, heaven was opened and the Holy Spirit descended on him . . .' (Luke 3:21,22). Those references are no more than selected instances of the uninterrupted flow of Jesus' hidden inner communion with the Father which energised his ministry.

The predominantly Jewish Christians in the first church quite naturally brought the practice of 'the three hours of prayer' with them into their new life. The second-century manual of Christian instruction on worship, the *Didache* (8:3), referring to the Lord's Prayer says, 'Three times a day you shall pray thus.' The Acts of the Apostles twice mentions prayer 'at three in the afternoon' (Acts 3:1; 10:3,30). When Paul says that he prays 'without ceasing – continually – day and night – always', he doesn't mean unbroken prayer around the clock, but the faithful observance of the tried and tested 'three hours of prayer'. It helps us to make practical sense of the puzzling instruction to 'devote yourselves to prayer' (Colossians 4:2) and 'pray continually' (1 Thessalonians 5:17) – puzzling because it suggests a schizophrenic attitude to life, with the mind half on prayer while driving, or handling machinery, crossing a busy road or bathing the baby. For working people '3 pm prayer' is hardly feasible, but even the busiest can find a corner somewhere in the soul to pray the Lord's Prayer.

Festival praise

The Gospels remind us of another side to Jesus' prayer life within Israel's traditions, the festivals when the people came together to enact their distinctive identity as God's covenant people. Professor David Ford writes on Hebrew Festival celebration:

Worshippers are deeply involved physically, dancing, shouting, prostrations, clapping, singing and feasting. It was an experience with many dimensions, rich and concentrated, and in the Psalms distilled yet further into poetry.[2]

Picture how Jesus threw himself into the excited drama of the Feast of the Passover riding on a donkey among the Hosannas of the great seething crowds (John 12:12–16). Just as he could at any moment withdraw into the still, secret places of the heart to commune with his Father, so also he was at home in the big occasions of national rejoicing, turning Israel's memories of salvation into prophetic affirmations of even greater things to come. Have we allowed the power and meaning of our own festivals to bleed away under secular pressures?

Without private prayer, we condemn ourselves to superficiality; without vibrant, public worship we exclude ourselves from enacting our distinctive identity as God's redeemed servant people, agents of his kingdom in a dark world. Jesus held both together, private and public as one. The desire to glorify the Father creates 'one place, everywhere'.

The distinctive Jesus

What is special, unique about Christian prayer? 'One day Jesus was praying in a certain place. When he finished, one of his disciples said to him, "Lord, teach us to pray, just as John taught his disciples"' (Luke 11:1). The disciple wasn't implying that until that moment they had never prayed. They were Jews and practised the 'three hours of prayer' long before they met Jesus. He was asking for the Christian's trademark prayer. Disciples of John the Baptist, and in various other religious groupings, had their own prayers; what sets Christian prayer apart from the rest? Jesus answered with the Lord's Prayer, and a new way of praying was born (see p 29).

'The Lord's Prayer is an Aramaic prayer . . . the invocation of God as Abba coined by Jesus is also Aramaic, as is the final cry from the cross (Mark 15:34). Thus Jesus not only prayed in his native tongue in his private prayer, he also gave his disciples a form of prayer couched in the vernacular when he taught them the Lord's Prayer. In doing so he removed prayer from the liturgical sphere of sacred language and places it right in the midst of everyday life.'[3] He restored prayer to the people, by calling on Almighty God, 'the blessed and only Ruler, the King of kings and Lord of lords, who alone is immortal and who lives in unapproachable light, whom no-one has seen or can see' (1 Timothy 6:15,16), as 'Abba, Father!' 'Abba' stems from the speech of children, and is unique to Jesus in addressing God. It is the core of his own faith in God. Moreover, the evidence that we really are children of God will be seen in the way we say, after the Holy Spirit, 'Abba!' (Galatians 4:6; Romans 8:15,16). And only the Holy Spirit can make 'Abba' not merely a name to be repeated but a God to be trusted, as a child runs into the arms of her mother.

'Abba' unlocks a vision and an interpretation of life. Nowhere in his teaching did Jesus stop to defend the Father or explain the reasons for his actions in the world: the name 'Abba' is all the explanation, interpretation and defence of the ways of God required. Plunged into the fog of events, wondering where God might be in the confusion and what he is up to, Christ's totally reassuring message is delivered in the one word 'Abba'. Faced with life's usual anxieties, Jesus is able to convey peace and optimism into our minds with the bedrock truth that 'your heavenly Father knows' (Matthew 6:31–34), and that if *he* knows, then it doesn't matter greatly if we don't know. That is the logic of knowing how to call God our 'Abba, Father'. Once we surrender to its wisdom and allow it to patrol our inner world, with unhindered access to every room in our anxious minds, we learn to laugh again with the 'carefree seriousness' of confident children.

'I know not what the future holds, but I know who holds the future', and his name is 'Abba, Father'. Not politicians, market forces, occult forces, but 'my Father'. That is a masterful way of praying through daily life, in which we are content to know nothing (of God's secret ways of answering prayer) – but at the same time knowing everything, in knowing God's best name, 'Abba'.

Jesus himself, as he tells us, learned to trust in God as Abba. When he commends the Father to us as worthy of our confidence and obedience, it is out of his own experiential knowledge. In a wonderful saying he refers to the custom in Jewish society of a father teaching his son the family craft. Behind locked doors (to guard the family trade secrets from possible competitors) the father will pour into the boy everything he knows: how to handle tools, how to select and fashion wood and stone, how to make a fishing net or the boat, etc. The future of the family's business is passed on to the son. Jesus was the Father's apprentice:

> At that time Jesus said, 'I praise you, Father, Lord of heaven and earth, because you have hidden these things from the wise and learned, and revealed them to little children. Yes, Father, for this was your good pleasure.
>
> 'All things have been committed to me by my Father. No-one knows the Son except the Father, and no-one knows the Father except the Son and those to whom the Son chooses to reveal him.'
>
> Matthew 11:25–27

and because of the skills he learned in secret from the Father, Jesus is able to offer rest to the weary and burdened (vs 28–30).

From the other characteristics of Jesus' way of praying, we mention just one.

Dominated by thanksgiving

It need not surprise us that our prayer should dominated by thanksgiving, when we think of the significance of our address to God as 'Abba, Father'. Well-brought-up children know how to say 'thank you'. The prayer we have just quoted is the only prayer of Jesus quoted at some length, and verse 25 opens with 'At that time Jesus said, "I praise you Father. . .".. Glance back at what had just happened 'at that time' (vs 20–24) and we see it was the failure of his message and miracles to move the cities to repentance. His prayer is thanksgiving in the face of failure! Similarly, when he raised Lazarus from the dead in the presence of broken-hearted relatives, Jesus began his prayer to God, 'Father, I thank you that you have heard me' (John 11:41). He gives thanks before he has made his request! The dominance of praise and thanksgiving throughout Jesus' prayer is full of profound significance, because thanksgiving is one of the great signs of the new age. A Jewish saying from the first or second centuries AD goes as follows:

> In the world to come all sacrifices will cease, but the thank-offering will remain for ever; likewise all confessions will cease, but the confessions of thanks will remain for ever.

When Jesus gave thanks in spite of failure he was confessing that God is Lord over all, regardless of appearances to the contrary; praise claims the hopeless situation for God. When he gave thanks for prayers answered, even before he had spoken his prayer, he was claiming God's future reign now. Those who pray 'Your kingdom come' can go on to participate in its answer by thanksgiving at all times and in all circumstances. Praise, particularly praise in the dark, is profoundly defiant and prophetic. It is saying 'What we see happening is not the last word – the will of God is the last word, so much so that I will now thank you Father for glorifying your name at this time.' Praise puts each situation into true light. Hence the command for each ordinary day is:

> Be joyful always; pray continually; give thanks in all circumstances; for this is God's will for you in Christ Jesus.
>
> 1 Thessalonians 5:16–18

By thanksgiving we taste 'the goodness of the word of God and the powers of the coming age' (Hebrews 6:5). It isn't in the least surprising when the world falls into gloom – it has plenty of reasons for so doing – but it is a scandal whenever the church of God mirrors those attitudes, forgetting its calling and the reason for its existence, which is to witness to the reality of the new age. Thanksgiving is the language of such witness. 'A Christian should be an alleluia from head to foot' (Augustine).

Questions for reflection and discussion

1. Daniel's defence against the Babylonian threat to his devotion to God was more prayer (p 70). He protected his mind against fear and compromise through prayer three times a day. How are you applying his example to your own life?

2. The picture of Jewish festival praise, which was part of Jesus' tradition of celebration (p 71), raises the question, 'Have we allowed the power and meaning of our own festivals to bleed away under secular pressures?'

3. Jesus gave thanks to the Father *before* he made his requests (pp 74, 75). Set yourself to practice praise-led praying today and notice how this approach transforms your view of the Lord's presence in your affairs.

Chapter 8

'FEED THE GAPING NEED OF MY SENSES'

I have a persistent mental picture of this book as a convoy of coal wagons delivering their load to a power station where it is swallowed up and converted into energy. All very efficient, but with no allowances made for the personal moods or needs of the workers. Thus we see chapter on chapter of these reflections about the great business of prayer and our communion with God, which the reader is expected to swallow and convert into energy – though you and I know that spiritual life is not as simple as feeding coal to a power station.

Prayer isn't a self-contained engine. It is inextricably bound up with the sort of people we are, with our fluctuations, the highs and lows of our fickle inner weather and, yes, the question of our personal holiness. Who hasn't known times when gaps open up in their praying, when the flow of prayer-thought and of prayer-language stutters intermittently and jams? Patrick Kavanagh expressed his personal longing for a revitalised prayer life, as fresh and boundless as spring after a hard winter.

> Feed the gaping need of my senses, give me ad lib
> To pray unselfconsciously with overflowing speech
> For this soul needs to be honoured with a new dress woven
> From green and blue things and arguments that cannot be proven.[1]

That is a beautiful but risky request, 'give me ad lib to pray unselfconsciously with overflowing speech', for it is a far deeper business than mere improved prayer technique. In fact, it is a request which will cast us into crisis for, by implication, it invites the Lord to do a thorough cleansing of the life from all the impediment to prayer-thought and prayer-speech. Thankfully, for us, the praying people featured in the Scriptures were in this respect no different from ourselves. They were not flawless, stainless paragons of personal holiness, but they struggled with similar experiences of failed prayer. One man in particular was plunged into a crisis over what he called his 'unclean lips', which blanked out his communion with God.

But first, by way of preparation for our encounter with Isaiah, a word about cattle in the Scottish Highlands. Unaccustomed to a sight of the sun during long winter months, they are inclined to go slightly berserk whenever it does manage to break through the gloom. The moment is called a 'sun-blink' and we mention this piece of bovine trivia here only because it was an experience akin to a sun-blink which altered Isaiah's approach to God.

Glowing coals on the altar of incense created a twilight atmosphere in the Jerusalem temple, which suited Isaiah's mood as he reflected on recent political upheavals (Isaiah 6:1–7). The nation awaited a new word from God, and who was to communicate that word but Isaiah. If at that moment he was immersed in the details of his task, what happened next left the man shattered. Suddenly, as if projected onto the clouds of incense, a dazzling sun-blink of God's glory burst through the gloom:

> I saw the Lord seated on a throne, high and exalted.

Why this and why now?

Just when the prophet needed all the encouragement and support possible for his crucial and possibly dangerous ministry, he is pulverised by a vision of the divine majesty. In our reflections on the Lord's Prayer (see pages 29–48) we came to the conclusion that the reason why the first three petitions were exclusively concerned with the glory of God is because things go best when he is honoured with first place.

The first spiritual law is always 'Seek first his kingdom and his righteousness, and all these things will be given to you as well' (Matthew 6:33). Had the prophet, under pressure of events, compromised that principle? Perhaps he had lapsed into 'managerial' mode, in the same way church leaders today can be fascinated by strategies which promise 'results' and 'success' but do not necessarily 'seek first the kingdom'. Were Isaiah, and the school of prophets, as much prone to pragmatism and the art of influencing people as we are today? Evidently something was out of kilter for God to burst in on him in such a devastating manner. Apparently Israel's greatest need at that moment was for Isaiah's personal holiness.

The instinct of self-glorification is imbedded in the texture of our being, and so close to its centre that we can hardly catch it happening. If, as with the great Isaiah, it takes a sun-blink of God's glory to shock us to our senses, then let us beseech the Lord for a whole volley of them. Over and around the vision move seraphs (the word means 'glowing beings of light'), acting as a protective screen against dangerous radiation from the divine presence. Yet even those glorious beings 'covered their faces' against the unbearable splendour of the vision. What Isaiah sees extends to his hearing and the seraphic hymn of cosmic adoration which rocked the temple (v 3):

> Holy, Holy, holy, is the LORD Almighty;
> the whole earth is full of his glory.

Yet there is still no affirming word to the prophet; in fact, so far, no word directed to him at all; *still* the scene is dominated by angelic fascination with God's glory and holiness; and still the prophet's motives and aptness for ministry are further exposed to scrutiny. The good news here is that it appears we are not, after all, mere functionaries in the kingdom, operatives good only for running errands and little else. We *do* matter! So much so that the Lord will not leave us to our spiritual mediocrity, to wallow in our third-rateness. Isaiah was bursting to be out on the job with

God's message to the people, but his first need was to be trans-fixed by the realisation of God's holiness and its corollary that God's people are called to be 'holy as he is holy'.

The small, familiar word 'holy' carries a huge load of work, for it must convey an idea of God's total perfection. Applied to the prophet's sphere, as well as to our own, 'holiness' is the norm which God requires in us. When he pronounces creation to be 'very good' (Genesis 1:31) he meant 'it is exactly what I mean it to be'. In the church where I preached last Sunday, after the service members went out into the adjoining market crowds with cheerful invitations for people to come in for soup. It was, surely, a 'holy' act, just the sort of thing God intends his people to do. 'Sin', therefore, is whatever departs from the creator's norm. 'Holiness does not exist in mystic speculations, enthusiastic fervour, or uncommanded austerity; it consists in thinking as God thinks, and willing as God wills.'[2] The fact that God wants holiness for us and believes that we are, by grace, capable of holi-ness is a miracle. 'The greatest miracle that God can perform today, is to take an unholy man out of an unholy world, and make that man holy and put him back into that unholy world, and keep him holy in it.'[3] We are, each of us, candidates for miracle.

God's holiness and glory are twin attributes. We can have knowledge of one only via the other. They are two aspects of the divine reality – not so much two sides of the one coin as the outside and the lining of the same coat: 'Holiness is God's hidden, concealed glory ... but his glory is his holiness revealed.'[4]

When lips are 'unclean'

Desperately casting around for ways of expressing an idea of God's unique and literally incomparable nature, we say rather limply that 'God is totally other'. Not that he is separated from us 'up there' or 'out there' in space and time. He is 'other' than we are and separated from us as wind is separated from a vacuum or light from darkness. A Hebrew poet, meditating on the contradictory emotions we experience at any serious attempt to look into the face of God, found it a baffling conundrum. We cannot endure the sight of that face, yet life is not truly liveable without it:

> Lovely face, majestic face, face of beauty, face of flame . . .
> Whoever looks at him is instantly torn; whoever glimpses
> his beauty melts away . . . for their strength fails and their
> faces are charred, their hearts reel and their eyes grow
> dim at the splendour and radiance of their King's beauty.[5]

In spite of the trauma of the revelations bursting in upon Isaiah at that moment (revelations of God's holiness and his own impurity), it was also the sanest moment of his life:

> O how shall I, whose native sphere
> Is dark, whose mind is dim,
>   Before the ineffable appear,
>   And on my naked spirit bear
>   The uncreated beam?[6]

Isaiah was stripped of all illusions about his achievements and merit as a prophet. Any self-aggrandisement vaporised in that light. As he approached God's norm for a human being, he was approaching holiness.

> 'Woe to me!' I cried. 'I am ruined! For I am a man of unclean lips, and I live among a people of unclean lips, and my eyes have seen the King, the LORD Almighty.'
>
> Isaiah 6:5

A prophet whose lips are put out of commission by personal defilement is a contradiction in terms. We can only speculate at what lay behind that despairing cry. Was he conscious of misusing his gifts? Or compromising on his message? Perhaps some arrogance or complacency in his approach to his work? False

vows, perhaps, or idle vows? But we have quite enough to do
with our own unclean lips:

> With the tongue we praise our Lord and Father, and with it we curse
> people, who have been made in God's likeness. Out of the
> same mouth come praise and cursing. My brothers and sisters, this
> should not be. Can both fresh water and salt water flow from the
> same spring?
>
> James 3:9–11

Jesus set enormous importance on the words we speak. He
rejected the conventions governing foods – kosher and prohib-
ited – on the grounds that dangerous defilement isn't affected by
what we eat but by what comes out of our mouths in our words
(Mark 7:14,15). So, guard against even the casual thoughts,
unkind or insulting terms like 'Raca', meaning blockhead, or
'You fool!' – which, disturbingly, he brackets along with murder!
(Matthew 5:21). Any words of ours which smear, slander, spread
doubts or judge another person Jesus forbids outright.

Not only so, but Jesus teaches us to trace our speech back to
its origin in the heart:

> Good people bring good things out of the good stored up in their
> hearts, and evil people bring evil things out of the evil stored up in
> their hearts. For out of the overflow of one's heart, the mouth speaks.
>
> Luke 6:45

'Unclean lips' in Jesus' analysis, occur when we speak words
surging up from a store of 'unclean' thoughts and out into circulation. Once out they cannot be recalled again, the damage is
done and will go on being done by those words let off the leash.

Or was Isaiah's sense of guilt and defilement more simply an
awareness of 'fallenness' and of a life biased away from God,
habituated to sin? The irony, indeed the absurdity of his posi-
tion may have rushed in on him at that moment. There he was,
a miniscule human being, proposing to do business with the

All-Holy One – like a flea going into partnership with a mammoth, or a leaf snatched up by a passing hurricane, or even like an Inverness cow driven crazy by a sunblink on Christmas Eve. Perhaps he saw some humour in the fact that God was vastly too great to be captured within the vision, for Isaiah saw no more than the train of God's robe filling the temple. Sitting there, a prophet struck dumb by personal failure, a worshipper unable to pray, a preacher unable to proclaim to the people, Isaiah was 'ruined'.

The seraphs' song merely served to exacerbate his misery, for those radiant beings know nothing of the believer's split-mindedness. They are as they sing, wholly consecrated to God, with clean, uncompromised lips, their motives transparent and, in a proper sense, simple. But sin silences praise. The psalmist experienced similar struggles as he attempted to frame adequate words in praise and witness. In his case, his lips seemed stuck, unable to move. Like Isaiah, he too realised that it wasn't a matter of a visit to the speech therapist, for only the Lord can mend our impaired speech and release our lips for song, prayer and testimony:

> O LORD, open my lips,
> and my mouth will declare your praise.
>
> Psalm 51:15

Diagnosis and healing

In biblical symbolism, the mouth (lips, tongue, speech) represents the whole person, because our complexity of language is one of the features that distinguish humanity from other creatures. Thus the psalmist sees the fulfilment of life in 'lips' that are occupied with their highest work in God's praise:

> My lips will shout for joy
> when I sing praise to you –

83

> I, whom you have redeemed.
> My tongue will tell of your righteous acts all day long . . .
>
> Psalm 71:23,24

This joy fills life and exposes 'unclean lips' as a disaster causing the person, or congregation, to miss their intended purpose. Isaiah saw very well the implications of his condition and declared himself 'ruined', for praiseless lips are an appalling waste. For that same reason the psalmist explains to God that death is not a good idea for, 'Who praises you from his grave?' (Psalm 6:5), a question which waited the resurrection of Jesus for an answer.

The wasting condition of 'unclean lips', which are too defiled to utter worship, is rooted in the reign of the self. When our so-called and much celebrated 'free will' turns out to be not so free after all, but is in fact self-will, lips are defiled by self-enslaved speech. So much for the diagnosis; what of the cure? We can no more reach, purify and revitalise our own speech than we can 'take out our eyes to look at them' as one writer puts it. For Isaiah, slumped in despair at the devastating disclosure of reality, healing and renewal came from beyond himself when 'one of the seraphs flew to me with a live coal in his hand, which he had taken with tongs from the altar. With it he touched my mouth and said, "See, this has touched your lips; your guilt is taken away and your sin atoned for" ' (Isaiah 6:6,7). Isaiah offers himself up to God in response: 'Hear am I, Send me!' (v 8) and at once he is commissioned with urgent words: 'Go and tell this people . . .'

The prophet who now leaves the temple is not the same man who came in earlier. His prophet's knowledge and expertise are pervaded by a profound experience of God as the 'consuming fire' and he has found it to be a fire of examination and judgement, but also of grace. He emerged imprinted by that encounter; his cleansed lips able now to speak words of truth and mercy. We are led to wonder by this event if the church can have an authentic prophetic ministry unless it undergoes something like Isaiah's encounter with God. He came out with a profound sense of God's holiness and saving grace; he knew death and resurrection in his own experience and as such he incarnated the very message Israel needed to hear. Can our own witness to holiness, judgment and regeneration be authentic without having experienced them, not only into our minds or our theology but also into our bodies? Can we speak to our world unless our own lips have been touched and cleansed? Testimony, to be authentic, requires the unstrained naturalness of overflow. The over-brimming joy and gratitude of personal discovery of God's grace, which cannot be faked, is the prerequisite of testimony. Who God is, what he has done and what he is doing lead on to surprise, discovery, possibility, delight, reassurance and praise – which become the starting point of mission.

Isaiah's discoveries raise questions for us: What, in our case, is the cleansing and revitalising of unclean lips by a 'live coal from the altar'? Can the dreary cycle of defilement-cleansing-defilement be broken and replaced by consistent holiness? What, or who, can keep us cleansed and open to God in a way that delights him? Is it possible to live and pray in communion with God free from constant preoccupation with our own spiritual state? Our sense of need in these matters is real; how real is God's answer? In exploring God's response to our questions, the next chapter will bring us to the heart of worship.

Questions for reflection and discussion

1. What, in our case, is the cleansing and revitalising of 'unclean lips' by a 'live coal from the altar?'
2. Do you agree with the idea that 'holiness' is not primarily a refraining from certain practices but rather thinking and willing as the God of love thinks and wills? (p 80).
3. Jesus and the importance of speech: When did you last deliberately 'store up good' in your heart so that it might 'overflow' in the way you speak? (pp 82, 83). Is there something in this chapter which you might take and 'store up'?

4. Spend some time in prayer for your church asking for 'unclean lips' to be cleansed and restored, perhaps asking for a 'sun-blink' of God's holy love.

Chapter 9

DUET: THE CHILD AND THE DIVA

While I was listening to a talk, a sentence came hurtling across the room like a live hand-grenade and landed on my brain. The explosion altered my understanding of worship. The speaker had said, 'The trouble for many Christians is that they have only half a Saviour.' If his intention was to be provocative he succeeded brilliantly in my case. Subsequent discussions clarified the speaker's meaning as follows. We can think of Christ's ministry to his people as having two aspects. First, he saves us from sin, and, secondly, he saves our worship and prayer from failure. Our road to the Father's home is routed through the cross; our road to true, acceptable worship is routed through Christ's own worship. He redeems our defiled worship and ineffectual prayer as much as he redeems our lives from the power of sin. By routing our poor worship through his own rich worship he is able to offer both, his and ours, as one to the Father.

The speaker's point was that we trust Jesus to reconcile us to the Father through the cross and forgiveness of sins, but then we go on to act as though the matter of prayer and worship is up to us. We lay tremendous stress on Christ as Saviour from sin, but not as the brother whose worship vitalises our offerings (see pages 13,14 'Prayer and the DIY Fallacy'). I felt the speaker had exposed a real weakness in our usual practice of prayer. I still do. Is this the reason why worship and prayer are often such hard going and, if we are honest, at times something of a disappointment?

Whose worship needs redeeming?

Isaiah's traumatic vision of 'unclean lips' in the service of the holy God demonstrates how our own thoughts, words, actions and offerings must undergo a process of continual cleansing and renewal if they are to reach the Father's presence. Look, for instance, at our preoccupation with styles, trends and traditions of worship. We move among them hoping to discover the thing that will work the trick and help our congregation to achieve spiritual and emotional lift-off. Of course, you could equally argue that the great variety of ideas and materials in the worship-industry is a sign of energy and creativity, suggesting a desire to be the best we can for God; to emulate the psalmist's cry 'Let everything that has breath praise the LORD . . .' (Psalm 150:6).

However, there does seem to be a certain amount of nervousness and insecurity concerning the effectiveness of our efforts. What we offer up on a Sunday morning may reach and move the congregation – but does it reach and move heaven? Either we are dissatisfied and restless over our worship, never sure if it makes any real difference; or we are just as likely to give ourselves the benefit of the doubt, secretly convinced that God will be rather grateful for all the trouble we take to praise him. Yet again we may have forgotten that scene where the great Isaiah, stunned witless by a glimpse of his dire need before God, sits crying something about being 'ruined'.

By definition, in worship we must get ourselves out of the way; to be free from our usual mixed and murky motives, able to give all our attention to gazing towards the face of the Father.

Patrick Kavanagh wrote:

> Me I will throw away . . .
> . . . To go on the grand tour
> A man must be free
> From self-necessity.[1]

To which we mutter 'if only' and 'but how?' Where will we attain sufficient freedom from self to go on the 'grand tour' with God? There is a way, and it is the only way. If we desire to give to God the best our hearts can offer, yet be free from endless self-analysis of the quality of our worship, we must allow our prayer to be born again within Christ's prayer.

This is because it isn't possible to tell the spiritual worth of a particular act of worship. We are more confident when concerning ourselves with the 'outside' of worship: with style, order, procedure, selections, though even here our estimations cannot escape personal bias. Surely we will have every sympathy with the minister or worship-leader determined to awaken the congregation from the lethargy of over-familiarity with predictable forms week after week. Yet familiarity is not synonymous with stupor. CS Lewis argued for the spiritual worth of the well-known and well-tried. He suggests that services 'work best when, through long familiarity, we don't have to think about it. As long as you notice, and have to count the steps, you are not dancing but only learning to dance. A good shoe is a shoe you don't notice. Good reading becomes possible when you do not consciously think about eyes, or light, or print, or spelling. The perfect church service would be one we were almost unaware of; our attention would have been on God.'[2]

The debate continues. For some, set forms are a tyranny, the kiss of death to any hopes of inspiration by the Holy Spirit during the service. Others will agree with the man who complained of certain 'innovative ministers', 'I wish they'd remember that the charge to Peter was "feed my sheep"; not "try experiments on my rats", or even, "teach my performing dogs new tricks"'. Difficult. This issue sends us back behind appearances and felt responses, to connect with the fundamental principle that when Christ saves, he saves *completely*. First, he saves us from the dominion of sin; but he doesn't then leave us to our own devices, with a little help from the Holy Spirit; for he adds his own worshipping, praying life to ours, drawing our praise and prayer into his own and so to the Father. With this astounding idea we reach the wellspring of communion with God.

The wise Christian will move in with this truth, pondering its biblical expressions deeply and habitually, allowing it to direct and regulate his devotion.

'I, yet not I'

Consider Paul's words about a Christian's union with Christ as the dynamic of communion with God:

> I have been crucified with Christ and I no longer live, but Christ lives in me. The life I live in the body, I live by faith in the Son of God, who loved me and gave himself for me.
>
> Galatians 2:20

On the one hand there is my normal, ordinary 'life I live in the body', and on the other there is 'Christ' who 'lives in me'. What of the other 'I'? The 'I' of the unclean lips and the sin-biased heart, the 'I' of the defiled worship and compromised service? That 'I', the 'old I', is no longer the controlling principle within the Christian's life, since it has been 'crucified' in union with Christ. The new principle is 'Christ lives in me' in a union fashioned by Christ's self-outpouring love for us, and energised by the Holy Spirit of Jesus dwelling in us. What, if we may so express it, is the indwelling Christ doing in and with us? He is saving our lives from failure, taking our devotion and prayer into his own, in a reconciling exchange. He takes on our life and we take on his.

Another translation/interpretation of Galatians 2:20 strikingly clarifies the insight of the verse when it suggests 'The life I live in the body, I live by faith, the *faithfulness* of the Son of God who loved me and gave himself for me.'[3] According to this translation, our union with Christ does not depend upon the strength and consistency of *our* faith in him, but by his unalterable *faithfulness* in giving himself wholly to us for our whole redemption. Such truths are utterly fundamental to our communion with the Father.

Christ the Mediator

In biblical symbolism the Israelite High Priest mediated the relationship between God and people (Hebrews 5:1–3). So valuable is the old symbolism that, even as the letter to the Hebrews cele-brates the redundancy of the old covenant priesthood, the author retains its imagery and prophetic symbolism as the best way of teaching Christ's superiority! The mediating High Priest ministered the things of God to the people, and the things of the people to God. All communion, both ways, passed through the Mediator who represented the 'many-in-the-one' and 'the-one-for-the-many'. Was Israel's worship accepted by God? Keep your eye on the Mediator. Did God come to the people? Again, keep your eye on the Mediator.

When the Mediator enters the presence of God, he is the 'One' representing 'the many'. When he prays, all Israel prays in him; when he offers the blood of atonement for sins, all Israel offers in him; when he intercedes for the harvest and the cattle, all Israel intercedes in him. It is as though the people, waiting outside the holy place of the divine presence, were stretching out their hands to touch the Mediator. In fact the names of the twelve tribes were embossed on his vestments so they stand before God when he stands before God, the many in the one. When he worships God, all Israel worships in him, through his mouth. The people's prayer is only as effective as the Mediator's prayer. As he is before God, so are the people. They are on his heart; he cannot move, speak or act without taking them with him. Mediator and people are as one.

Bringing that symbolism forward to Christ and the church, we have a stunning disclosure of the effectiveness of Christ, our Mediator, when he prays. We, the many, throughout the world, are gathered into Christ the One. Our offerings are enfolded within his offerings. As Christ is with God, so are we with him. But notice one vital difference between the symbolic high priest of Israel and the reality of Jesus. Israel came to God *through* their mediating priest; we come to God not only through Christ but also *in* him. There is a vast world of grace in that small prepo-sition. We pass *through* a door and leave it behind as we walk on; but we live all day *in* the clothes we wear. By faith we 'wear' Christ, we are in him (Galatians 3:27). Our status before the

Father is as assured as Christ's! We might say that we are 'wearing Christ' because we are 'in' him; the Father cannot see us (in all our imperfections) because of Christ who covers us. When Jesus mediates for us as high priest, he acts *vicariously*, taking our place so that we might have his place before the Father. This means that Christ steps into every situation when we are required to enact our faith and trust in God. At that moment (be it the moment of prayer, worship, service, witness, healing, loving) we see Jesus praying, worshipping, serving, witnessing, healing, loving, on our behalf and in our place.

Such a reconciling exchange is possible only because God in Jesus became a true man, one of us, our brother. Thus he is able to substitute his humanity for our humanity. His worship is offered to the Father out of his life as a man, and therefore it can touch and transform our own offerings. Our worship and prayer in and through Christ depend absolutely on the fact that he wasn't a superman, or even an angelic man, but a man like ourselves. When heretical teachers in the early church denied Christ's humanity on the grounds that Almighty God could never reduce himself to be born of Mary, the orthodox teachers responded with their great war-cry, 'What Christ did not assume, he cannot heal.' Our belief that Jesus heals our lives does not depend primarily on the accounts of his healing miracles in the gospels, but on the fact of the incarnation, when he 'assumed' (took on) our humanity, healing it by living from within it to the glory of the Father. At last! A real man has appeared in the human family to represent them to the Father. No wonder Martin Luther called Jesus 'the proper man'.

The Duet: the Child and the Diva

How does our prayer relate to, and connect with, Jesus the Mediator's prayer? I like to picture it as a child (ourselves) singing at the Covent Garden Opera House, before a vast and knowledgeable audience. She is very nervous, her voice is weak and off-key, her legs are trembling with fright, and she can hardly remember her words. This performance will be a shambles. Then onto the stage comes a great diva and, far from sending the child packing, takes her by the hand and together they sing a duet. The superb voice and the small voice, it is a duet, two people are singing here. As they sing, the child's voice gains confidence, picked up on her partner's great voice and thrown out to a delighted audience as one voice. Our Mediator does not leave us to sing solo. '. . . He is able to save completely those who come to God through him, because he always lives to intercede for them' (Hebrews 7:25).

Applying that analogy to our prayer and Christ's prayer, the two voices synchronise, in the Spirit.

The synchronising Holy Spirit

Take an instance of synchronised prayer, ours with Christ's in the cry 'Abba, Father'. We first meet with the address when Jesus instructs his people to say with him, 'Our Father' (Matthew 6:9). The second time we meet it, the Holy Spirit enters our minds urging us to open our mouths and call on God as 'Abba, Father' (Romans 8:15,16). On the third occasion we become the place in which the Holy Spirit of the Son prays '*Abba*, Father': 'Because you are his children, he sent the Spirit of his Son into our hearts, the Spirit who calls out, "*Abba*, Father"' (Galatians 4:6). Thus the Holy Spirit is the one who synchronises, harmonises and coordinates the mind of Christ with our minds, in a wonderful duet.

There is still more in the image of the duet between the child and the diva. The way we have described it, the child was singing alone and the diva joined in. A sweet idea, but theologically it must be the other way round! Before we think to utter a word of prayer our Mediator is already ahead of us, praying our prayer for us (as it should be prayed). Although we like to imagine ourselves as initiating worship and prayer in the mistaken idea that prayer doesn't exist until we decide to pray, the Mediator is already about his task of taking our place before the Father. 'Every high priest . . . is appointed to represent [the people] in matters related to God . . .' (Hebrews 5:1). Unlike the reclining Buddha in the caves at Yala in South Thailand, whose devotees must awaken him with fireworks and gongs to get his attention for their intercessions, Christ 'always lives to intercede' for us (Hebrews 7:25). We participate in the worship and intercession which Christ and the angelic hosts are offering ceaselessly day and night.

When we awaken in the morning the truth is that, regardless of our mood, the room is alive with Christ's worship of the Father with 'the thousands upon thousands of angels in joyful assembly' (Hebrews 12:22). Isaiah, as you will recall, felt the foundations of the temple shuddering with the angelic adoration. Therefore, clearly, our first concern in coming to prayer is to prepare to participate in the Mediator's praise and intercession for the world. We will confess our sins and claim the gospel promise that the 'blood of Jesus, his Son, purifies us from all sin' (1 John 1:7). We will ask the Holy Spirit to attune our minds to, and synchronise them with, Christ's prayer to the Father. Then we will quietly listen for whatever the Spirit suggests to our spirit as the burden of our own prayer, which is also the Mediator's prayer.

Thus we place ourselves within the flow of the Holy Spirit, who comes out from the mind of the Father into the mind of the Son and so to the mind of Christian people:

> . . . The Spirit searches all things, even the deep things of God . . .
> no-one knows the thoughts of God except the Spirit of God. We
> have not received the spirit of the world but the Spirit who is from
> God, that we may understand what God has freely given us . . .
>> 'For who has known the mind of the Lord
>> so as to instruct him?'
> But we have the mind of Christ.
>
> 1 Corinthians 2:10–16

Even a child may sing with a diva! And when the two voices mutually interpenetrate each other in a duet, what anxiety is lifted from the smaller voice. The child no longer need worry about the success of her performance, for that responsibility has been taken over by her partner with the great voice. Allow yourself to accept the freedom that comes when Jesus the Mediator covers our life with his in every respect. Free, now, for spontaneous joyful response and worship and service. All that remains for us to do is to deny ourselves and take up our cross and follow him (Matthew 16:24).

Questions for reflection and discussion

1. Discuss with your congregation the suggestion that 'the trouble for many Christians is that they have only half a Saviour' (p 87).
2. Is it the case that we trust to venerable traditions, or new styles of worship, 'to discover the thing that will work the trick and help our congregation to achieve spiritual and emotional lift-off' (p 88)? Consider what it would mean in our Sunday worship, if we believed that Jesus has already 'worked the trick' and he is, in himself, our 'spiritual and emotional lift-off' to the Father. In worship what is his part and what is our part?
3. Do you know any people of other faiths? Invite them to describe to you their 'mediator' in their approach to the deity. Then describe to them Christ the Mediator (p 90–92).
4. Take time to ponder, and embrace the marvellous 'Duet' which Christ sings with us, to the praise of the Father (p 92, 93). Now practise it, by allowing the Holy Spirit to lead your prayer into Christ's prayer.

Chapter 10

THE INSIDER

The vitality of our communion with God lies in the hands of the Mediator: in his hands, his mind, his faithfulness, his achievements. He is our worship before the Father, offering his worship as ours. Our words are taken up into his words, to be cleansed, unscrambled, interpreted and raised to a higher power as they mingle with the Mediator's voice and are offered to God.

Yet even as we are praying, an anxiety may come bubbling up from the depths asking, 'How well does Christ know us?' Can we trust him to know us so thoroughly that we need never put on an act in his presence? Prayer might be the one place in all creation where we can be totally honest, without any pretending, because nothing about us could surprise our Mediator. What a vast relief that is! So, how well does he know us? Consider three observations:

> Our Lord Jesus knows how to ride the lame horse; he can carve the rotten wood.
>
> Martin Luther

> A God who was a mason and a carpenter for thirty years can surely make short work of the ruins of my soul.
>
> Urs Balthasar

> The Mediator must be 'able to deal gently with those who are ignorant and are going astray, since he himself is subject to weakness'.
>
> Hebrews 5:2

The lame horse, the rotten wood, the ruined soul, the ignorant, the wayward: these are the sphere of the Mediator's expertise. Consider his extraordinary gifts of sympathy, his depth of insight into our darkest regions, and his mastery of the realities of our existence, which he could attain only by immersing himself in our life. To answer our question, Christ the Mediator knows his people with the knowledge of full experience.

Experience is the truest knowledge

All else is theory. A psychologist describes how, when writing a book on loneliness and its effect on people, she came up against the awkward fact that she had never personally been seriously lonely. To her great credit she learned to sail solo sufficiently well to take her boat across the Atlantic. By the time she stepped ashore in the US she had acquired an intense, life-changing experience of loneliness which qualified her to speak of the condition. Her patients surely noticed the difference, and her book will have the authority of personal experience.

Perhaps the word we are searching for as we distinguish between theoretical and experiential knowledge is 'taste'. No amount of book knowledge can convey the essence of a taste. When people who have lived in the tropics attempt to describe to the uninitiated the sensation of eating that strange fruit called durian, the verbal contortions can be comic. 'At first it smells like a drain and tastes like extremely old socks, but persist and you'll realise you are eating the favourite fruit of the angels.' Or, more simply, just get hold of one and taste it! When Christians try to explain the reasons for their commitment to Christ, they soon reach a point where the best they can do is to emulate the man who advised his friends to 'taste and see that the LORD is good' (Psalm 34:8). An ounce of insider knowledge is worth a truck-load of the other sort.

The Father asked his Son to 'taste and see' what it's like on the inside of these lives of ours, and so qualify himself to become our

Mediator. The great New Testament passage which unlocks this truth, so fundamental for our confidence in communion with God, is Hebrews 2:10–18.

> In bringing many sons and daughters to glory, it was fitting that God, for whom and through whom everything exists, should make the author of their salvation perfect through suffering.
>
> Hebrews 2:10

We say of someone who has come to our assistance, 'That was just typical of him. If you knew him, you would realise it is just like him to be so generous and helpful.' Here the writer says 'it was fitting' or, it was typical of him, to be so wise and compassionate in the way he brings 'sons and daughters to glory'. Before a single son or daughter had started out on the journey, God had provided the one thing essential for success, a 'pioneer of their salvation', where 'pioneer' means leader, or pathfinder, able to bring his people through a dark and hostile world.

It is puzzling to read that Jesus 'the pioneer' required to be 'made perfect', when we believe him to be the perfect, sinless Son of God. How is it possible, and why should it be necessary, to improve on perfection? It was a matter of qualifications for the Mediator's job. He must be 'able to deal gently with those who are ignorant and are going astray, since he himself is subject to weakness' (Hebrews 5:2), a skill only acquired by years, in the laboratory of human experience. For that reason, 'Since the children have flesh and blood, he too shared in their humanity . . . he had to be made like his brothers and sisters in every way, in order that he might become a merciful and faithful high priest in service to God' (Hebrews 2:14–17). It is our humanity that he takes into the presence of God. The only way the Son of God could qualify, himself and so be entrusted with the success of our lives as we journey home 'to glory', was by subjecting himself to our weakness.

Hence the surprising way he prepared himself for the duel with Satan, which would set the rhythm for the rest of his mission

(Luke 4:1–13). He deliberately weakened himself; through fasting he lowered his energy levels until he could experience within himself the full blast of demonic testings, the subtle, seductive, plausible whispers which so ruined Eve and Adam. This was solidarity-without-pretending, genuine fellow-feeling with us in discipleship. Check your own experiences of temptation against the three Jesus faced in that encounter.

Look out for the surprising fact that each testing attacked Jesus *at the point of his greatest strength*: his compassion, his commitment to the Father, and his trust in the Father. Satan was devilishly cunning in appealing to Christ's strength in order to deflect him into doing not the Father's but the Satanic will. If we dare say that God, until that moment, knew all about the ways and wiles of Satan 'theoretically', in Jesus he would now 'taste' the experience for himself.

1. Compassion was a sign of the Messiah who would feed the hungry (John 6:30–33). But now he was himself hungry (Luke 4:2) and felt in himself what the cravings of the senses, particularly hunger, can do to a human being. It is very difficult to keep in focus the higher claims of the will of God when the stomach is empty. Full of sweet reasonableness, the devil suggested that hunger is never a good thing and that as the Son of God he should really take care of his health for the sake of his ministry. Anyway, 'providing bread' is Messiah's work. And if literal hunger through lack of food is, thankfully, not our immediate problem, the principle stands: physical and material desires, in the attitudes of our culture, override the spiritual. 'What is the will of God?' gives way to 'What do I feel like?', which ignores the fact that we are made in God's image and reduces us to one of the beasts. The message is pumped out with quite demonic persuasiveness that we must not deny ourselves, we must not go without. With an empty stomach, Jesus took into himself the torture of physical desire yet maintained that 'people do not live on bread alone' (v 4).

2. The second temptation was the offer of instant celebrity, attainable without the fearful cost of doing the will of God at the cross (vs 5–7). Did Jesus come to redeem and claim the world? Satan will give him the world (an authority which Jesus didn't question): 'If you worship me, it will all be yours.' But to trust God means we trust his way of doing things and leave 'results' to him. Haven't you felt the powerful attractions of spiritual short-cuts? For instance, the natural tendency is to want society's approval for what we do. To be regarded by the world as reasonable people who just happen to like a little religion. 'Nice' people. In that way churches can become everyone's friend, or is it everyone's pet poodle? But mission is *God's* mission in which his priorities must be our priorities. The gospel has huge, searching, scary things to say to society en route to announcing the forgiveness of the cross. We are not allowed to bypass the tough things in our rush to reach the 'good' part of the gospel. If we find this difficult (and who doesn't), be assured that Jesus discovered in the most uncompromising way possible how hard it is to 'worship the Lord your God and serve him only' (v 8).

3. The third test was about proving to himself that God was still God, by asking him to demonstrate his divine power. Turn on the booster rockets just to show that they still work. Jesus was invited by Satan to prove his own trust in the Father by diving off the pinnacle of the Royal Porch of the Jerusalem temple, a sheer drop of 450 feet into the Kidron valley below. 'Anything is possible to him who believes', so why don't we amaze the world with a show of our faith and God's faithfulness? Provide spectacular evidence and so convince the doubters. Jesus rejected the suggestion by insisting that our business is to trust God, not to test him (v 12). If we are trusting him as Jesus intends, we will not need to test God, neither will every puzzling difficulty be a crisis, a make-or-break moment for our faith. Nevertheless, Jesus felt the power of temptation to put on a show to prove his faith in God.

Diagnostic knowledge

Through such engagements with the forces of evil (and the three temptations recorded in Luke would be no more than a typical sample of how Jesus was 'made perfect through what he suffered'), Jesus entered, felt, tasted, and took fully into his body and mind our spiritual conflicts with the demonic. With his first-hand experience of what we are going through on our journey, the Mediator can feel the vibrations of our heart, to decode our words, cries and sighs. To qualify, he was required to walk our path, a step at a time, to become totally acquainted with all our temptations.

Jesus did the unimaginable when, as Urs Balthasar said, 'he opened himself to Satan's fascination in order to burst the dazzling bubble from within.' How reassuring it is to know that the One who mediates our relationship with the Father has himself tasted temptation and found it fascinating and even dazzling. Against the seductive, fascinating and debilitating suggestions that we would be happier if we gave up on the will of God, we have the power and the wisdom of the Mediator available to us.

Jesus emerged from his apprenticeship in human experience with profound, hard-won, inner knowledge of his people. He had engaged with Satan and, wishing to 'enter a strong man's house and carry off his possessions', he had first tied up the strong man (Matthew 12:29) – meaning that he penetrated to the demonic depths of human existence. He knows all about 'the fury and the mire of human veins' (WB Yeats), having suffered cruelly because of it. He is able to read every nuance of our reaction to temptation. 'Because he himself suffered when he was tempted' with a suffering which was essentially like ours, 'he is able to help those who are being tempted' (Hebrews 2:18). He brought back with him not merely knowledge but a *diagnostic knowledge* of the spiritual oppression and bondage that a person may be under, and of where to apply healing and release. His prayers for his people are guided by his profound knowledge of our condition.

To be able to minister to our needs, Jesus entered the mysterious depths where the demonic disrupts creation, both physically and spiritually. To the lame man he says, 'Friend, your sins are forgiven' (Luke 5:20). Concerning a troubled woman he says, 'Then should not this woman, a daughter of Abraham, whom Satan has kept bound for eighteen long years, be set free on the Sabbath day from what bound her?' (Luke 13:16). 'Jesus knows how to ride the lame horse; he can carve the rotten wood.'

> Both the one who makes people holy and those who are made holy are of the same family. So Jesus is not ashamed to call them brothers and sisters.
>
> Hebrews 2:11

He is our brother in every way (Hebrews 2:17). In the tradition which is the background to Hebrews, calling Jesus 'our brother', and for Jesus to call us 'brothers and sisters' in the same family, means he is our Goel. The term means the strong relative who would come to the aid of family members in trouble. He was duty bound by blood ties to deal with their problems, bail them out of prison, redeem them from slavery, fight their enemies and make their problems his personal responsibility – and he isn't ashamed to have such relatives or such a family.

Our part is to put our full weight on the relationship, to call on him for help, to look to him to bring us through. In terms of verse 11 our burden concerns our unholiness. Holiness means to live in the way the Lord desires, for which we need all the help Jesus, our Goel, can supply.

Two further images follow:

In the first, Jesus says, 'I will declare your name to my brothers and sisters; in the presence of the congregation I will sing your praises' (Hebrews 2:12). The words are quoted from Psalm 22:22, at the turning point in the Psalm. David turns from describing a grim time on the run from King Saul (vs 1–21) to gratitude and praise at God's wonderful deliverance. David foreshadows Jesus, who went down into darkness and death but was brought from death by the power of the Father. David is pictured standing among 'the assembly', bearing testimony to the Father's faithfulness and urging his 'people' to put all their trust in God. Take the picture forward to Jesus standing among the church, sharing his experiences of God's saving grace with us and urging us to trust in the Father as he did.

The second image is from Hebrews 2:13:

> . . . 'I will put my trust in him.'
> And again he says,
> 'Here am I, and the children God has given me.'

This is another striking image of Jesus' inseparable closeness to us. The words are Isaiah's at a time of crisis in Israel, under attack from Assyria (Isaiah 8:17,18). The prophet has two children. One is named as a grim warning of Assyrian conquest, 'the spoil speeds'; the other lad is named as a promise of restoration for Israel, 'a remnant will return'. Now picture Isaiah (the name means 'God saves') standing before Israel's leaders holding his boys' hands. They are the message, of warning and deliverance. Now apply that to Christ and his people, standing before an unbelieving society. With him ('I and the children God has given me'), we are the message of both judgement and hope.

This succession of brilliant images gathers around the central figure of Christ as the mediating High Priest and the conclusion that, because of the immense achievement of his incarnation, he is 'able to help those who are being tempted' (Hebrews 2:18).

We have celebrated Christ's solidarity and sympathy with his people, which express the human face of the mediator. Yet, as we well know from ordinary life in the world, although sympathy is always welcome it can be powerless to help. If I have a heavy cold, and you also have a bad cold we sympathise entirely with each other but neither of us can help the other. Jesus' sympathy, in contrast, flows from the 'throne of grace' (4:16). Sympathy backed by sovereignty is an omnipotent sympathy, able to achieve in us what Christ the Mediator desires for us. And it is the greatest incentive for delight, praise and confident prayer.

Questions for reflection and discussion

1. Jot down a list of those people you regard as 'insiders' with you. What do they have, as far as you are concerned, that the 'outsiders' don't have?

2. Jesus took his insider 'diagnostic knowledge' of us back to the Father (p 101). What difference does that fact make to the way we pray? How long and how detailed need our explanations to him be of the way we feel?

3. Call to mind those particular temptations which are too fascinating to be resisted (p 100). Visualise them as a 'dazzling bubble' which mere advice or exhortation cannot touch. Now visualise Jesus going beyond advice, teaching and exhortation, reducing himself to the point where he 'opened himself to Satan's fascination . . . to burst the dazzling bubble from within.'

4. Satan attacked Jesus by appealing to his greatest strengths (p 99). Does that suggest that 'playing to your strengths' is not necessarily the same thing as doing the will of God on particular occasions? Can you think of instances of this in your own experience, and in the life of your church?

Chapter 11

PRAYING THE COVENANT

Adolf Hitler's opinion of spiritual life is well known. He dismissed conscience as 'a Jewish invention' and announced to his people that 'Heaven is for sparrows and Christians! We'll take the world.' To the secular mind, prayer appears a fragile, ephemeral business when measured against the powerful systems and institutions that drive society. Christians are asked if prayer actually connects with anything real and solid in the here-and-now world, or is it simply a self-perpetuating activity within the enclosed life of church and devotion, designed chiefly to lift the spirits of the faithful?

It is a fair question, and best dealt with by returning it straight back over the net with a confident forehand smash. By all means apply the test of 'reality' to prayer and to the entire sweep of Christian faith. Thus we might ask Hitler if he still believes he was wise to root all his ambitions in the 'solid reality' of the here and now? At the moment of writing (December 2004) the world is reeling from a shocking parable on that question posed by the tsunami in the Indian Ocean. Entire coastal and island populations have been obliterated; the death toll is rising daily. After the initial shock to the senses as we try to take in the magnitude and the appalling suddenness of the onslaught, there came a more reflective shock for those of us who pass through life trusting to its steady reliability and our culture's mastery of nature's forces. The assumption of our invincibility was exposed as a myth. Life is precarious and transitory, although we like to imagine it well founded and permanent. One moment vast numbers of people had their lives firmly in their hands, the next, those hands lie lifeless and in many instances all trace of their existence has been washed away.

To transcend the transient

The cynic may dismiss the parable I am attempting to draw from the catastrophe on the grounds that, living in Pitlochry, he is well out of reach of Asian tsunamis, so far. It is not in any way to trivialise the physical horror of the event if we take that eruption on the floor of the Indian Ocean as symbolic also of our own vulnerability to personal disruption. The tectonic plates under our seemingly stable existence can shift suddenly, 'earthquake' experiences occur without rhyme, reason or warning: sickness, bereavement, tragedy, failure, isolation, loneliness, breakdown in family or other vital relationships, infidelity, injustice, unemployment, humiliations are only some of the tremors.

We are not blaming transience! Life is transient. From birth to maturity to decline and death is the rhythm that makes the world fascinating, risky, mysterious, and wonderful. The point of these remarks is to question the wisdom of trying to *build and anchor one's life on what is transient.* In his parable of the two houses (Matthew 7:24–27), Jesus describes two very different types of men with the same aim: to build a strong, weatherproof house. One man took enormous trouble to construct his house on a foundation of rock. For the other man sinking holes into the rock was far too laborious and unnecessary, so he erected his house straight onto sandy soil – which looked solid enough in dry weather. Suddenly came the only test that matters: storms and flash floods. The rock-based house stood steady while, of course, the other one collapsed. Jesus adds the comment that 'it fell with a great crash' (v 27). The crash of hopes, the collapse of self-respect as neighbours witness the debacle, perhaps also injury to his family trapped in the wreckage. More than just a setback, it was 'a great crash' as plans for the future come to nothing. Jesus raised the possibility of life's tsunamis and left his audience, now, as then, with choices to make concerning rock or sand, life founded upon what is transitory, or a life that transcends the transitory and connects with the eternal.

Our essential life, if it is to realise its promise and fulfil it's meaning, must be rooted in the eternal. Jesus claimed that quality for his own word. It is not wise to put roots down in the transient here and now, because when it goes, life goes with it. Jesus, again, expressed this truth in terms of the 'treasure' in a person's life (Matthew 6:19–21). If the treasure (the focus) is earthbound, limited to the transient here and now, when it goes (moth, rust, theft) it takes the heart with it, because 'where your treasure is, there your heart will be also' (v 21). But if your 'treasure' is in seeking and doing the will of God, it will be 'stored in heaven', taking your 'heart', your essential life, with it.

Only the life which is rooted in the eternal will be free enough from the distractions and the limitations of the here and now – its myopia, and the way it is so easily dazzled by each new thing – to handle it wisely, allowing it proper place and value. Only those who have vital connection with the eternal know how to live, freely and responsibly in the present. Simone Weil said as much in her aphorism that 'To be always relevant, it is necessary to say things that are eternal.' Is prayer 'relevant'? Does it connect with 'reality'? Nothing is more relevant or more connected with reality than Christian prayer, offered to the Father, through the Son, in the Spirit, for by its nature it is locked into God and the eternal. True relevance requires that we are 'coordinated with eternity' which, in the first chapter, was our definition of prayer (p 15).

Prayer is like the umbilical cord leading from the child of faith into the source of her nourishment and growth in the eternal God. To the secular mind, the difficulty of the idea of life sustained through a prayer-communication line into the life of God is that it vanishes out of sight into the invisible realm. True, and while thanking God for every gracious manifestation of the presence and the gifts of the Holy Spirit in our times of prayer, decisive evidence for its efficacy comes not from phenomena but from what God has promised. We are well aware of the evil one's ability to counterfeit spiritual manifestations, with his own version of 'signs and wonders' (see instances of his ability to perform 'great signs' in Revelation 13:11–18).

By faith in God's promises, prayer connects us with the eternal, taking our essential life with it. Not faith as in 'Have you passed your exams? I hope so', implying a desperate trust in miracle. Rather, '. . . Faith is being sure of what we hope for, and certain of what we do not see' (Hebrews 11:1). Mere invisibility is no problem to this faith, because it doesn't depend upon phenomena and observation but upon God's word. This faith doesn't begin with a list of 'things I can just about believe' and then work out and up towards God, checklist in hand. This faith stands before God in simple, honest acknowledgement that we haven't a clue about how a human being might transcend the transient and ground his life in the eternal in God. This faith holds that it is utterly reasonable to begin with God (not try to work towards him!); indeed, it would be lunatic arrogance to do anything else.

This faith is teachable and open to receive God's astounding self-revelation as one who establishes his relationship with us on a covenant basis and, therefore, it is utterly dependable.

[13]When God made his promise to Abraham, since there was no-one greater for him to swear by, he swore by himself, [14]saying, 'I will surely bless you and give you many descendants.' [15]And so after waiting patiently, Abraham received what was promised.

[16]People swear by someone greater than themselves, and the oath confirms what is said and puts an end to all argument. [17]Because God wanted to make the unchanging nature of his purpose very clear to the heirs of what was promised, he confirmed it with an oath. [18]God did this so that, by two unchangeable things in which it is impossible for God to lie, we who have fled to take hold of the hope offered to us may be greatly encouraged. [19]We have this hope as an anchor for the soul, firm and secure. It enters the inner sanctuary behind the curtain, [20]where Jesus, who went before us, has entered on our behalf. He has become a high priest for ever, in the order of Melchizedek.

Hebrews 6:13–20

Praying the covenant

When God makes a promise, that, surely, should be sufficient for faith. But because we have learned to be wary of promises, we look for some binding reinforcement that the promise-maker cannot escape. You will recall games in the school playground when a promise or a vow was only valid if clinched with a blood-curdling oath. My own most solemnly binding oath was, 'I swear on my mother's deathbed' although she was alive and well at the time!

Knowing our spiritual insecurities, God condescends to enter our little oath-binding games. You can read a vivid account of just how far he went, in the Semitic covenant-making rituals, to prove to Abraham the rock-solid unbreakable nature of his commitment (Genesis 15). The point is, God knows we need assurances from him. But assurance cannot be stronger than our assurance of God himself. Whenever we pray, the question is lurking around 'can I be sure of God?' First, he gives himself to us in a promise of life and salvation, and then he double-strengthens that promise with an oath sworn by the highest presence in the cosmos, 'himself' (Hebrews 6:13–15). Thus the invincible logic of the new covenant relationship is described as 'by two unchangeable things in which it is impossible for God to lie, we who have fled to take hold of the hope offered to us may be greatly encouraged' (v 18).

Christian prayer is alive with hope drawn from the huge resources of the 'two unchangeable things' of the new covenant. We believe it to be as strong as the character of God, as irreversible as the incarnation, as powerful as the cross, as certain as the resurrection, and as immediate to us as the Holy Spirit. The sum effect of praying from within the new covenant assurances is 'hope' which we have as 'an anchor for the soul, firm and secure'. But on what does the anchor actually anchor? On God. 'It enters the inner sanctuary behind the curtain where Jesus, who went before us, has entered on our behalf' (vs 19,20). It was, you remember, questions about the 'reality' of prayer, and whether prayer connects with anything real, which launched us into this reflection. Now we have our answer.

At the nerve-centre

Once again, the rich symbolism of Israel's old tabernacle and temple illuminates our need for strong assurances in prayer.

The 'inner sanctuary' was symbolically the holiest place of God's presence. Here the mediator brings the people to God, and here he receives God's blessings and words for the people. If we are searching for that point in the cosmos where prayer acts, moves and works, it is here in the person of the mediator, out of sight, behind the veiling curtain of the holy place (v 19). There Christ 'entered on our behalf'. He is the personification of our hope, which goes out to him, seeks him behind the curtain where he ministers for the world, and clings to him. Thus our prayer is anchored in the everlasting certainties of the new covenant and its mediator, Jesus Christ.

Already our faith is connected with God's ordained goal for our lives, in eternity. Therefore the characteristic quality of such prayer and worship is hope. Paul could pray for the churches:

> May the God of hope fill you with all joy and peace as you trust in him, so that you may overflow with hope by the power of the Holy Spirit.
>
> Romans 15:13

Where, in this society of ours do we turn for hope, real hope – big, compelling, overflowing, hope? In a recent letter a friend mentions that, 'the great missionary statesman, Lesslie Newbigin, once said, on returning to rich, privileged England from India, the thing which struck him most about this country was "a lack of hope". That was about twenty years ago but it could still apply today.' Christians often despair at the decline of faith, but in fact society is awash with 'faith' in the most extraordinary things, causes, ideas, personalities. But where is the hope?

Boundless hope, the state of 'overflowing with hope' arises from the knowledge that life is grounded and rooted in what is beyond sin, corruption and death, transcending mere transience, and embedded in the everlasting God. Because in a profound sense we have in Christ already reached 'home', we can travel this world with joy and gladness. For this reason we hear believers say wonderful things, like Lady Julian's, 'All shall be well, and all shall be well, and all manner of thing shall be well.'[1] That is the language of hope. Some are irritated by what they take to be the easy triumphalism of Julian's vision, but in fact it is a profound expression of new covenant confidence. Jürgen Moltmann writes that 'God is our final hope because we are his first love.'

The prayer of hope, hopeful prayer, arising from our entrance, with Christ, into the presence of God, 'the inner sanctuary', is a marvellous testimony to our world searching for something truly hopeful to hang on to. Far from apologising for the supernatural nature of prayer, we will gladly share its secret with others.

Praying for 'Sister Moon and Brother Sun'

Heaven alone gives ultimate meaning to our short-view hopes in this world. The hope of 'a new heaven and a new earth' (Revelation 21:1) means that our present 'small' hopes have somewhere to go; they flow like tiny streams towards the ocean of God's everlasting presence. Notice, however, that 'heaven' includes the fulfilment of God's covenant commitment to the created order (see Genesis 8:20–22 and 9:12–17). We pray for a *new earth* as well as for a *new heaven*, a promise confirmed by the *bodily* resurrection of Jesus from the dead, which is God's glorious 'yes' to creation. Thus our concerns are forced wide open by the new covenant to include intercession and praise for the created order. It means that we will dispense with that falsely over-spiritual disregard for the created world, which treats it like a crumbling launch pad from which, we hope, our spaceship will

111

safely blast-off and take us to glory! Our hopeful, hope-inspired, intercessions will extend to God's servant-creation, which also 'lives in hope' of resurrection:

> The creation waits in eager expectation for the children of God to be revealed. For the creation was subjected to frustration, not by its own choice, but by the will of the one who subjected it, in hope that the creation itself will be liberated from its bondage to decay and brought into the glorious freedom of the children of God.
>
> We know that the whole creation has been groaning as in the pains of childbirth right up to the present time.
>
> Romans 8:19–22

Paul's vision leads to Francis of Assisi and his ecstatic thanks-giving for God's creation. Here are verses from his 'A Song of Brother Sun', a joyous outpouring of a grateful affection for our world home. It deserves its place within our own prayers.

> A SONG OF BROTHER SUN
> Most High, all powerful, good Lord,
> to you be praise, glory, honour and all blessing.
>
> Only to you, Most High, do they belong
> and no one is worthy to call upon your name.
>
> May you be praised, my Lord, with all your creatures,
>   especially brother sun,
>   through whom you lighten the day for us.
>
> He is beautiful and radiant with great splendour;
> he signifies you, O Most High.
>
> Be praised, my Lord, for sister moon and the stars:
> clear and precious and lovely,
>   they are formed in heaven.

Be praised, my Lord, for brother wind
   and by air and clouds, clear skies and all weathers,
by which you give sustenance to your creatures.

Be praised, my Lord, for sister water,
who is very useful and humble and precious and pure.

Be praised, my Lord, for brother fire,
   by whom the night is illumined for us:
he is beautiful and cheerful, full of power and strength.

Be praised, my Lord, for sister, our mother earth,
   who sustains and governs us
and produces diverse fruits
   and coloured flowers and grass.

Be praised, my Lord,
   by all those who forgive for love of you
and who bear weakness and tribulation.

Blessèd are those who bear them in peace:
for by you, Most High, they will be crowned.

Be praised, my Lord, for our sister,
   the death of the body,
from which no one living is able to flee;
   woe to those who are dying in mortal sin.

Blessèd are those who are found doing your most holy will,
   for the second death will do them no harm.

     Praise and bless my Lord and give him thanks
     and serve him with great humility.

Francis of Assisi[2]

Questions for reflection and discussion

1. Look through the chapter once again, noting down a list of 'strong assurances' why we can trust God with our lives and with our prayers. Which of the 'assurances' do you find particularly satisfying?
2. Memorise the 'unchangeable' things (v 18) of Hebrews 6.
3. Do you agree with the comment that our society is 'awash with "faith" . . . but where is the hope?' (p 110). What do your friends 'hope in' and 'hope for'? Dare you point out to them the real (inevitable) likelihood of a 'tsunami' disruption coming out of the blue? (p 105,106).
4. Find a spot where you can see sky and earth. Using Francis's song (p 112,113), call upon creation to join with you in adoring the creator.

Chapter 12

CONTEMPLATIVE PRAYER:
A DAZZLING WORLD

A glance through the 'spirituality' section in the high-street bookshops will confirm that the trend everywhere is towards 'care of interior life'. At one end of the spectrum it amounts to little more than massaging moods. So, 'Allow yourself a leisurely soak in a scented bath among floating candles, with aromatic incense perfuming the atmosphere evoking Xanadu on a balmy evening. Put on Enya sweetly crooning and, relax. Now, can't you feel the stress just draining away?' More serious people are turning to various meditation techniques derived, originally, from Buddhism and adapted for exhausted Westerners. I recall a discussion with a Buddhist monk in a Thai temple in which we tried to explain to each other the aims of our respective religions. With what was a rather brilliant visual aid (I have never forgotten it) he filled a glass with water from the well and held it up to show the sediment swirling around in it. He explained that if he could hold the glass perfectly still for, say, an hour the sediment would start to settle. Hold it motionless for a day, a week, a month and the water would become crystal clear and transparent. The object of his meditation was not worship, or intercession, but to hold the 'glass' of his deepest mind still to allow for purification, illumination and serenity.

One reason for the new concerns about the interior life is not difficult to see: it is a desperate attempt at personal survival within the shredding machine which is everyday life for many people. Everything is up in the air, fast-changing, unrooted, superficial, media-soaked. It amounts to a conspiracy against the life of the soul. The lethal impact of modernity on religion has been well-labelled 'acid rain of the spirit', hence the desire to clear some space for the soul to breathe. We are rediscovering the riches of meditative and contemplative prayer.

Teachers of Christian spirituality warn of a number of obstacles opposed to interior prayer thrown up by the prevailing culture of modernity.[1] Three, in particular, which we will note before proceeding to think about contemplation and meditation: Narcissism, Pragmatism and Restlessness.

Narcissism

Narcissus was the famously good-looking lad who one day saw his own reflection in a pool and immediately fell in love with himself. Completely obsessed with himself, he inevitably reduced to become a little flower. Surely Narcissus is reincarnated in the mind and the attitudes of our culture, in the triumph of image over substance, style over content, spin over integrity. The extraordinary extent to which cosmetic surgery is now practised is another sign that Narcissus is alive and well. Vanity and egoism damage contemplative prayer by their preoccupation with personal freedom to choose whatever, and whoever we so desire. Our outlook is so filled with self-interest that we are quite unable to look for God within his creation, neither do we have the desire to. We are trapped within a thought world whose walls are lined with mirrors. In whatever direction we look we see only our own reflection. Consequently, the world of narcissism closes in, for we are not free enough from self-absorption to notice that 'the whole earth is full of God's glory' (Isaiah 6:3). Neither will we allow in any disturbing word from the Lord.

The personal catastrophe of excessive narcissism is in the way it shrinks the world to the level of our personal problems, anxieties and preoccupations. It is the polar opposite to the contemplative mind, since our attention is habitually routed through self-centredness. As a consequence, we cannot see or find God within the ordinary things of everyday life, which is, thereby, reduced to a spiritual desert.

Pragmatism

This is an attitude which is interested only in what works. It sums up our Western way of life, and clearly it is a successful approach to problem-solving which produces wealth and all manner of benefits for which we are grateful. However, it opposes prayer, and, in particular, contemplative prayer, by questioning their usefulness 'in the real world' (a favourite phrase of pragmatism). If you spend an hour cutting the grass, by the end you clearly have an hour's work to show for it; but what practical outcome can you point to for an hour's prayer? And because in our pragmatic culture our value and status depend largely on what we do, and are seen to do, where is the value in prayer?

Restlessness

Consider its opposite condition, 'restfulness' which 'is a form of awareness, a way of being in life. It is being in ordinary life with a sense of ease, gratitude, appreciation, peace and prayer. We are restful when ordinary life is enough'.[2] Restfulness doesn't mean passivity – it is not possible 'to be in ordinary life' without also being 'in' its opportunities, challenges and mysteries – but it is an acceptance of ordinary life as 'enough'. Is it enough? Apparently nothing is ever enough today, and it is virtually a confession of failure to say that 'ordinary life is enough'. The market and consumerism depend on their ability to draw us into a nervy restlessness in ordinary life, and we become impatient, insatiable, greedy for things and for experiences. We want to eat all the food, read all the books, see all the films, have all the partners, go on all the holidays, and the precious life-imparting sense of the presence of God is the first casualty. Compare our own spirit of restlessness, which is the death of contemplation, with David's deeply restful relationship with God (David, the man of tremendous action) in which a rich interior prayer life flourished:

> My heart is not proud, O LORD,
>   my eyes are not haughty;
> I do not concern myself with great matters
>   or things too wonderful for me.
> But I have stilled and quietened my
>   soul;
> like a weaned child with its mother,
>   like a weaned child is my soul within me.

Psalm 131:1,2

The contemplative mind

Consider Moses tending sheep on 'the far side of the desert' (Exodus 3:1). Same old flock, same old desert, just another boring, routine day in the back of beyond with zero prospects, and no hint of that day's extraordinary potential. Yet the episode also suggests that, in spite of the deadly familiarity of his circumstances, Moses was alert to his environment. Why else would he stand there in the heat, waiting for a burning bush to burn up? He was witnessing a miracle – but primarily that moment was a test. God wanted to know the qualities of this man; did he, like most of us do, pass through the familiar day half asleep, or was he expectant and open to new possibilities, God's possibilities?

First, the curiosity, the inquisitiveness, then the enquiry as Moses decides, 'I will go over and see this strange sight – why the bush does not burn up' (v 3). Only then does God speak to him from out of the flames. The incident reveals God's freedom to come to us how, when and where he chooses. Fire is not God, nor is it the glory of God, but in this symbolic and sacramental creation, fire is transparent to God. The writer of the book of Esdras said, 'Lord, your glory passed through the four gates of fire and earthquake and wind and ice, to give the law to the

118

descendants of Jacob' (2 Esdras 3:19). The burning bush was, at that moment, God's chosen gate for his appearing. Then he spoke. But notice how much mysterious activity had occurred before he spoke:

> . . . 'Moses! Moses!'
> And Moses said, 'Here I am.'
> 'Do not come any closer,' God said. 'Take off your sandals, for the place where you are standing is holy ground.'

Exodus 3:4,5

Elizabeth Barrett Browning's paraphrase of God's words gives a definition of the contemplative mind:

> . . . Earth's crammed with heaven,
> And every common bush afire with God;
> But only he who sees takes off his shoes,
> The rest sit round it, and pluck blackberries![3]

The first sphere of our contemplation is a creation 'on fire' with the glory of God. A creation which speaks of God, and which calls us to adore the Creator, ('Take off your sandals'). The believer will go into each day with a humble, expectant mind, a child-like mind in the sense that children are not yet blunted and dulled by custom, they are not yet under the deadly tyranny of unthinking habit. The contemplative mind looks into the day knowing that everything is touched by the fire of God's holy presence, and it is prepared to adore. In our spirits, if not physically, we kneel in submission before the fire. GK Chesterton said of the posture of kneeling:

The gesture of worship is generous and beautiful. We not only feel freer when we bend, we actually feel taller when we bow. Henceforth anything that takes away the gesture of worship stunts and even maims us forever. Henceforth being secular is servitude and inhibition. If we cannot pray we are gagged; if we cannot kneel we are in irons.[4]

A conduit of the divine

Many Christians today are discovering in Thomas Traherne (1637–74) a man for whom all things were 'holy ground'. He was convinced that the world is good and from his earliest days he found it beautiful:

> The world's fair beauty set my soul on fire.
> My senses were informers to my heart,
> The conduits of his glory, power and art.
> . . . and every sense
> Was in me to like some intelligence.

The ordinary world was, to his praising mind, a continuous, universal miracle. 'The most excellent things are the most common. Were there but one cup of water in all the world, a bushel of diamonds would be trash in comparison.'[5] Long before our ecological concerns, and our new respect for the created order, Traherne wrote these words:

> They rejoice in a piece of gold rather than the sun: and get a few little glittering stones and call them jewels. And admire them because they be resplendent like the stars, and transparent like the air, and pellucid like the sea. But the stars themselves which are ten thousand more times more useful, great, and glorious they disregard. Nor shall the air itself be counted anything, though it be worth all the pearls and diamonds in the thousand worlds. A work of God so Divine by reason of its precious and pure transparency, that all the worlds would be worth nothing without such a treasure.[6]

It is all there before us, waiting to be seen, if only we will cease to 'sit around and pluck blackberries' but remove our shoes and adore:

> We need nothing but open eyes, to be ravished like the Cherubim.[7]

And because it is a sacramental creation, the world speaks of God. It is a means of his self-revelation, a conduit of the divine. He comes to us through the beauty of the natural world.

The contemplative Traherne loved creation, or rather he loved the Creator in his creation. To such a mind, the smallest things also witness to God's wisdom as well as the cosmic infinities:

> Suppose a river, or a drop of water, an apple or a (grain of) sand, an ear of corn or an herb: God knoweth infinite excellencies in it more than we: He seethe how it relateth to angels and men; how it proceedeth from the most perfect Lover to the most perfectly Beloved; how it representeth all His attributes.[8]

Is it possible to love the created world too much? Traherne thought the greater danger lay in loving it too little, or in the wrong way:

> O what a treasure is every sand when truly understood!
> Who can love anything that God made too much?

The contemplative mind looks for the true value of things as 'conduits' for the love and wisdom of God:

> What a world this would be, were everything beloved as it ought to be.

Words which would serve well as a motto for the United Nations environment agencies.

This precious season

Two further things from the ecstatic-contemplative mind of Thomas Traherne. The first is the way he treasured the present time of this creation as a 'season in eternity'. We will live life now, with all the opportunity unique to a creation such as this, knowing that it is a phase within a greater, eternal life. We can do certain things now, in this 'season', before time is taken into eternity and faith and hope are fulfilled in sight. Heaven is another, a different 'season' with its own opportunities. The vital, contemplative mind understands that there is an appropriate way to live in the present 'season', of this creation. It matters what we do with it. Traherne urges his readers to enjoy the world, love the world and all creation, love one another, look at everything with the eyes of heaven, live a holy life, recognise and seize the present, unique opportunities:

> . . . it ought to be a firm principle rooted in us, that this life is the most precious season in all eternity, because all eternity dependeth on it. Now we may do those actions which hereafter, we shall never have occasion to do.

The contemplative believer will walk this world loving and valuing it for what it is, but aware that seasons change, heaven is up ahead. Thus he lives a full-bloodied life here and now, knowing that in this life all symphonies remain unfinished:

> So piecing this life with the life of Heaven and seeing it as one with all eternity, a part of it, a life within it: strangely and stupendously blessed in its place and season.[9]

The other insight from Traherne's contemplative understanding of a Christian's life in this 'season' is particularly intriguing. It falls into the category of things we can do now, in this season, that we cannot do in the next. It is that we return to God in praise for the wonders of this world, not only our words and the work of our hands, but the work of our imagination. 'The world within you is an offering returned', says Traherne, 'very delightful in flowing from him, but much more in returning to him', and this is because:

> God has made you able to create worlds in your own mind which are more precious unto him than those which he created . . . that power to create worlds in the mind is the imagination.

This puts contemplative prayer in a whole new light. The analogy which comes to mind is of a child's painting and bits of handiwork, of no value in themselves, but priceless to parents who delight to display them and boast of them to friends. For what most intrigues parents is 'how does my child see the world?'

Questions for reflection and discussion

1. For the next week keep a note of references to 'care of interior life' in the media and shops (p 115). What do they reveal of people's spiritual search?
2. Are you able to be sufficiently honest with yourself to recognise the presence of narcissism, pragmatism or restlessness? Can you discern the way they obstruct contemplative prayer?
3. How are progressive people to handle the statement that 'We are restful when ordinary life is enough' (p 117)?
4. We are not told how long Moses stood looking at the burning bush before he realised something extraordinary was happening (p 118). Are you able to keep yourself still enough, long enough to look at situations or events for their spiritual potential, as 'conduits of the divine'?
5. Discuss Chesterton's remark that 'our perennial spiritual and psychological task is to look at things familiar until they become familiar again.'

Chapter 13

CONTEMPLATIVE PRAYER:
THE FACE OF GOD

What do you see when you pray? You might answer that question and say that since we are saved by faith (not by sight), and we live by faith (not by sight), and we pray by faith (not by sight), what we 'see' doesn't come into it. But that answer would seem to make you more 'spiritual' than God himself who blesses his people by giving them a sight of 'his face':

The LORD said to Moses, 'Tell Aaron and his sons, "This is how you are to bless the Israelites. Say to them:
' "The LORD bless you
   and keep you;
the LORD make his face shine upon you
   and be gracious to you;
the LORD turn his face towards you
   and give you peace." '

'So they will put my name on the Israelites, and I will bless them.'

Numbers 6:22–27

It is, of course, a figurative way of speaking, a beautiful metaphor for the personal presence of God. He wants his people to know his presence not as blind, impersonal power but as personality. We read people's personalities chiefly in their faces. Prayer is essentially contemplative, because faced with the radiant face of God what can we do but gaze at him?

In the Old Testament the experience of God's presence was kept real and vivid by expressing it in simple, familiar, human terms, accessible in any language (anthropomorphic). The writers were prepared to risk describing God too closely by human terms, with the danger of transferring onto him our human limitations, for the sake of God's personal immediacy among his people. 'An unprejudiced evaluation of the Old Testament's humanising of the deity leads us to see, however, that in fact it is not the spiritual nature of God which is the foundation of Old Testament faith. It is his personhood – a personhood which is fully alive, and a life which is fully personal, and which is involuntarily thought of in terms of the human personality.'[1]

To the objection that the New Testament has superseded simple Old Testament anthropomorphism, we can point to the supreme statement of God's self-revelation in the New Testament: 'The Word became *flesh* and made his dwelling among us. We have seen his glory . . .' (John 1:14). God took his own figurative speech literally! In becoming flesh, he took on a face, a human personality which people could see, touch, hear, kiss, crucify, adore. Add to that Paul's observation that '. . . God . . . made his light shine in our hearts to give us the light of the knowledge of the glory of God *in the face of Christ*' (2 Corinthians 4:6).

We say of someone, 'it is written all over his face': whatever it was in his mind, before he could control it and frame words to express or suppress it, that thought or emotion had slipped the leash and displayed itself 'all over his face'. The face contains the eyes, the 'windows of the soul'. In some Far Eastern societies it is reckoned discourteous, as well as arousing suspicion, to wear dark glasses during a conversation. Inscrutable people, whose faces we cannot read, make us uneasy. It is in the power of a face to 'launch a thousand ships' and, even more impressively, to teach babies to smile by smiling at them. Babies are smiled into smiling. Is that another reason why God took a face?

In the Old Testament the face is always called the *panim*, in the plural, because of the various ways we can give our attention to another person. Our powers of doing so, through our organs of communication (eyes, ears, mouth) are arranged in the face. True worshippers 'seek the Lord's face'; they seek his presence before all else. It is our incredible privilege and calling to emulate the contemplative psalmist:

> One thing I ask of the LORD,
>> this is what I seek:
>> that I may dwell in the house of the LORD
>> all the days of my life,
> to gaze upon the beauty of the LORD
>> and to seek him in his temple . . .
> My heart says of you, 'Seek his face!'
>> Your face, LORD, I will seek.

Psalm 27:4,8

Contemplative prayer in the house of God

Again we encounter the wisdom of putting first things first (see p 30). 'Before you sew, first you must knot your thread.' Here the knot is the clear focus of 'one thing I ask of the LORD . . .'. Tourists visiting London will hope to visit many places and see many things, but their programme will be arranged around one essential experience, 'I absolutely *must* see Buckingham Palace'. Similarly, the psalmist longs to 'gaze upon the beauty of the LORD'. 'Gaze' implies a wondering, delighted scrutiny. 'Beauty' means not only the outward appearance of God's house but also the 'graciousness and pleasantness', the joy and satisfaction that derive from the Lord's hospitality in his 'house'. Another translation gives 'to behold the graciousness of the Lord and to visit early in his temple'. Where 'visit early' is to contemplate, suggesting someone who cannot wait to look again towards the face of the Lord, and to ponder the impressions aroused at the sight of him. 'That I may dwell in the house of the LORD all the days of my life' is figurative speech, meaning that he longs to be a personal guest of the divine host.

A metaphor, yes, but one which draws its power and shape from the physical experience of sitting in the house of God looking around at the signs and symbols of God's people's covenant identity (Psalm 73:15–17). Within those signs and symbols were reminders and promises of the Lord who 'makes his face shine upon you . . .', turning his face towards you in blessing. The psalmist gazed so as to penetrate to the heart of the symbols, signs and sacraments, shutting out all else in absorbed contemplation. In contrast, I'm inclined to think that many of our services have room for pretty much everything except contemplation.

Devotion wasn't always so unfocused. I was once minister of a small twelfth-century parish church which still displayed the iconography of Christ's wounds on the Rood Screen facing the congregation: the implements of Christ's torture, the crown of thorns, the scourging whips, hammer and nails, spear. Following the spiritual discipline known as 'Devotion to the Wounds', worshippers would prepare for Holy Communion by contemplating each wound in turn and what it will have cost Jesus to endure it; then they would turn reflection into prayer that the grace and power of the wounds might inflame the hearts of faithful people to love God.

Those worshippers saw the face of God in the face of the suffering Christ. In Isaiah's prophetic vision of the Saviour's face at the moment of crucifixion it was distorted beyond recognition:

> Just as there were many who were appalled at him –
>> his appearance was so disfigured beyond that of any human being,
>> and his form marred beyond human likeness –
> so will he sprinkle many nations . . .

> Isaiah 52:14,15

The medieval worshippers, who have so much to teach us about the suffering Christ, felt that the basic statement 'Jesus died for

127

our sins' should be received through long-looking, long-desiring, long-loving. It was through emphasis on the dreadful suffering of their Lord that men and women gained confidence to see in him a close brother. This form of devotion celebrated the sweetness, tenderness and accessibility of the truly human divine redeemer. The believer was emboldened to claim kinship with Jesus, whose wounds were a hieroglyph for his loving, intimate solidarity with people whose own lives were often grim and harsh affairs. Such contemplation became the dynamic for compassion towards others and a potent catalyst for mission. The sight of Christ crucified, in a painting, completely won over Zinzendorf the great missionary leader, whose motto became, 'Wherever at the moment there is most to do for the Saviour, that is our home.' His Moravians made it a matter of principle to go to the most deprived and marginalised. The love of God, revealed in the face of Jesus Christ, was poured into their hearts through the Holy Spirit (Romans 5:5).

'To look at him who is looking at you'

We are thinking about the prayer that arises within us as we contemplate the face of the Lord, meaning his personal presence. Before speaking comes the gazing which many of us find difficult. Ask us to shift a load of rocks as a sign of our love for the Lord and we will set about it straight away, but tell us to sit still and quiet for an hour contemplating the face of God and we will give you twelve reasons why we should be up and about doing 'useful' things. I am challenged by something Urs Balthasar wrote:

> Holiness consists in enduring God's glance. It may appear mere passivity to withstand the look of an eye; but everyone knows how much exertion is required when this occurs in an essential encounter. Our glances mostly brush by one another indirectly, or they turn quickly away, or they give themselves not personally but only socially. So too do we constantly flee from God into a distance that is theoretical,

rhetorical, sentimental, aesthetic, or, most frequently, pious. Or we flee from him to external works. And yet the best thing would be to surrender one's naked heart to the fire of this all-penetrating glance. The heart itself would then have to catch fire, if it were not always artificially dispersing the rays that come to it as through a magnifying glass. Such enduring would be the opposite of a Stoic's hardening his face: it would be a yielding, declaring oneself beaten, capitulating, entrusting oneself, casting oneself onto him. It would be childlike loving, since for children the glance of the father is not painful: with wide open eyes they look into his. Augustine's magnificent formula on the essence of eternity: 'To look at him who is looking at you.'[2]

Contemplating the Lord's face, his glance, his personal presence turned towards us, is not something we achieve through a series of psychological manoeuvres. Neither do we initiate it. Rather, we come into it, 'endure' it, and surrender to it. The urgent question arises: What are we meant to be looking at while under the Lord's radiant glance?

Remember one of our key scriptures:

> For God, who said, 'Let light shine out of darkness,' made his light shine in our hearts to give us the light of the knowledge of the glory of God in the face of Christ.
>
> 2 Corinthians 4:6

'The face of Christ' is revealed within our hearts by a sovereign creative act of God, only comparable to the 'let there be light' of Genesis (1:3). By the Holy Spirit we gaze upon the Lord in our hearts, calling into play everything we know of him 'in whom are hidden all the treasures of wisdom and knowledge' (Colossians 2:3). Paul goes on to say (v 4), 'I tell you this so that no-one may deceive you by fine-sounding arguments' about sub-Christian ways to the sight of God's face.

Therefore Christian contemplative prayer has nothing to do with emptying the mind, making it as blank as possible within, and waiting to see what happens next. The faith of the Old and the New Testaments is a prophetic faith, meaning reasonable communication between man and God for which the word of God to man, and man's reply, are crucial.

In the next chapter we shall think about 'meditative prayer' which arises out of a meditative use of Scripture. But the same Scripture teaches that the Lord in his sovereign freedom can reveal himself to us when, where and how he chooses. As we saw in the burning-bush episode, this symbolic and sacramental creation is a 'gate' through which the Lord can come to us. Therefore, a contemplative mind requires of us certain attitudes if we are not to miss the Lord's approach: attitudes of reverence, humility and submission towards the Lord-who-comes.

Reverence attunes the mind to God, putting the mind into an adoring frame appropriate to the presence of the Lord.

Humility keeps the mind pliable, teachable, grateful, expectant, open before both the familiar and the unfamiliar as potential 'gates' through which the Lord can come.

Submission is the acknowledgement that 'The fear of the LORD is the beginning of wisdom' (Psalm 111:10), and that we are dependant upon the Lord to feed the roots of our actions.

Contemplative prayer and the potential of the present moment

We shall mention two examples of how the Lord 'makes his face to shine upon us' from within his creation; how his personal presence can appear among us, through whatever medium he chooses to use.

1. Through music

Research into what it is that triggers in people an experience of 'God' reveals that 49 per cent mention *listening to music*. A young man writes:

A friend of mine persuaded me to go to Ely Cathedral to hear a performance of Bach's B Minor Mass. I had heard the work, indeed I knew Bach's choral work pretty well. I was sitting towards the back of the nave. The Cathedral seemed to be very cold. The music thrilled me ... until we got to the great Sanctus. I find this experience difficult to define. It was primarily a warning. I was frightened. I was trembling from head to foot, and wanted to cry. Actually I think I did. I heard no 'voice' except the music; I saw nothing; but the warning was very definite. I was not able to interpret this experience satisfactorily until I read, some months later of the 'numinous'. I was before the Judgement Seat. I was being 'weighed in the balance and found wanting'. This is an experience I have never forgotten.[3]

The music of John Taverner seems to convey the mystical nature of his Eastern Orthodox spirituality. It is as though by his music he is shaping an icon, 'a window of heaven'. The hymnody of such movements as Taize and the Iona Community evidently do something similar for many people. The living Lord can reveal his presence through our senses as well as through our reasoning minds. Christians in the past valued the sacredness of the senses, calling them the 'Talisman of the Lord', each one gifted to take some part in the mystery of creation. Our senses, as well as our minds and bodies, 'face' the Lord in contemplative prayer.

2. Through other faces

This is not as strange as it first sounds. The Lord can show himself to us through 'gates' of fire, and of music, and through the faces of beings created in his image.

This experience is like that of Jacob (Genesis 32:22–32) when he wrestled all night with a 'man' in the brook of Jabbok – except that the 'man' was a theophany, God-as-that-man. Jacob named the place Peniel, 'face of God', because 'I saw God face to face, and yet my life was spared' (v 30). Then

Jacob looked up and his worst nightmare was realised as he saw Esau, the brother he had famously swindled, coming up the road with a small army (Genesis 33:1). Jacob prepared to receive whatever revenge Esau had planned for him – but an extraordinary thing happened: '. . . Esau ran to meet Jacob and embraced him; he threw his arms around his neck and kissed him. And they wept' (v 4). There was not a word of recrimination, no reference to Jacob's deceitfulness. Esau's generosity of spirit overwhelmed Jacob, who, with his mind still full of Peniel, exclaimed, '. . . To see your face is like seeing the face of God' (v 10). The face of God in the face of a human being? Exactly. Look at Gerard Manley Hopkins' marvellous expression of this truth:

> As kingfishers catch fire, dragonflies draw flame;
> As tumbled over rims in roundy wells
> Stones ring; like each tucked string tells, each hung bell's
> Bow swung finds tongue to fling out broad its name;
> Each mortal thing does one thing and the same
> Deals out that being indoors each one dwells;
> Selves – goes itself; *myself* it speaks and spells,
> Crying *What I do is me: for that I came.*
>
> I say more: the just man justices;
> Keeps grace: that keeps all his goings graces;
> Acts in God's eye what in God's eye he is –
> Christ. For Christ plays in ten thousand places,
> Lovely in limbs, and lovely in eyes not his
> To the Father through the features of men's faces.[4]

Everything expresses its inward nature: birds, insects, bells and people. The Christian's inward nature means that he 'Acts in God's eye what in God's eye he is – Christ'. 'Christ-in-you' nature is stunningly expressed as 'Christ playing' in you. In fact he 'plays in ten thousand places' in people 'to the Father in the features of men's faces'.

Christ doesn't indwell us like an occupying force but as 'playing'. What might this mean?

In one of his books Stephen Prickett offers several intriguing suggestions:[5]

- Does Christ play in you as a *musician* plays?
- Or as an *actor*, expressing his life in the 'theatre' of your life?
- Or does he play in you as a *child* might play, as a game?
- Or is he playing in you as the *poetic mind* plays over its subject?
- Or as the sun plays on water?

Yes, all this and so much more besides, for 'he plays in ten thousand places', different in each unique person, lovely in their limbs and eyes, 'to the Father through the features of men's faces'.

Doesn't this consideration quite alter the way we look at other people, open to the possibility that Christ plays there?

To see your face is like seeing the face of God.

Questions for reflection and discussion

1. Make yourself comfortable, your space and your mind uncluttered, phones switched off. Read through Balthasar's words (p 128,129). Focus your thoughts on the line, '. . . the best thing would be to surrender one's naked heart to the fire of this [God's] all penetrating glance.' Refuse to disperse or deflect the rays of that glance. Be content to wait quietly, looking 'at him who is looking at you' (p 129). Prove for yourself that 'the heart itself would then have to catch fire'.
2. Have you had experiences similar to that Ely Cathedral encounter (p 131)? Music is one medium through which the Lord may choose to reveal his face. In your experience what are others? Are you able to speak of your experiences to other people?
3. 'To see your face is like seeing the face of God' (p 132). Pray for the expectation and the discernment to see the Lord's face in others today, and that they might see his face in ours.

4. 'Many of our services have room for pretty much everything except contemplation' (p 127). How is it in your own church? Is it reasonable to expect space for contemplative prayer in a worshipping congregation? Can we learn anything from medieval devotion (p 127,128)?

Chapter 14

MEDITATIVE PRAYER: 'THE SOUL IS DYED THE COLOUR OF ITS LEISURE THOUGHT'[1]

It isn't difficult to snip the nerve of the soul. A scalpel isn't necessary: simply refrain from contemplative prayer. Jesus' story about the 'banquet without guests' (Luke 14:15–24) can be read as a description of the non-contemplative life in which each invited person pleaded busyness with the perfectly legitimate activities of making a living and building a future. Work and busyness run parallel to another event going on at the same time, 'the great banquet' of love between host and guests celebrated with superb food and the best wine. The message is clear and timely: get control over the runaway busyness of your life by submitting the demands of work (and the clamour of leisure!) to the renewal that comes through worship.

A wise observer remarks that 'the life that is too busy for worship is busier than God intended it to be. Work is life's pre-eminent duty but worship is life's pre-eminent dynamic, for while work exhausts power, worship renews it.'[2] What sort of worship? Obviously, at our Sunday gatherings; but chiefly it is a spirit of worship throughout the day, the attitude and slant of mind by which prayer is as unselfconscious and habitual as breathing.

In his extraordinary sonnet, 'Prayer',[3] George Herbert coins 27 images of prayer, one of which is 'breathing':

> Prayer the Church's banquet, Angel's age,
> God's breath in man returning to his birth,
> The soul in paraphrase, heart in pilgrimage,
> The Christian plummet sounding heaven and earth;

Engine against the Almighty, sinner's tower,
Reversed thunder, Christ-side-piercing spear,
The six-days world transposing in an hour,
A kind of tune, which all things hear and fear;

Softness, and peace, and joy, and love, and bliss,
Exalted manna, gladness of the best,
Heaven in ordinary, man well dressed,
The Milky Way, the bird of Paradise,

Church-bells beyond the stars heard, the soul's blood,
The land of spices; something understood.

The sound of breathing

When he writes that prayer is 'God's breath in man returning to his birth', does he mean the Holy Spirit, or is it the physical breath in our bodies? Perhaps both meanings; yet I am drawn to the second interpretation. When we pray, our breath returns 'home' to the God who gave it, freighted with his praise. That is to say, the use of your breath in prayer and worship is its chief and most natural use. It completes the circle, from God into our bodies and back to him in prayer. The act of prayer ventilates the soul, allowing our breath to flow through us and out on its short homeward journey to God, for all the world like a child running to its mother's arms.

On the other hand, consider the stress placed on our spirits when we refuse prayer. Society would be happier if it accepted prayer as normal and as necessary to a person's health as the sun and rain, and not as a special, religious activity. Rabbi Lawrence Kushner makes a fascinating suggestion regarding prayer and breathing:

The letters of the name of God in Hebrew are yod, hay, vav and hay, they are frequently mispronounced Yahweh. But in truth they are unutterable. Not because of the holiness they invoke, but because they are all vowels and you cannot pronounce all the vowels at once without risking respiratory injury. *This word is the sound of breathing.* The holiest Name in the world, the Name of the Creator, is the sound of your own breathing. That these letters are unpronounceable is no accident. Just as it is no accident that they are also the root letters of the Hebrew verb 'to be' . . . God's Name is name of Being itself.[4]

To think that God placed the sound of his unknowable Name on the breath of every person! It is a beautiful sign of the Creator's closeness to his children. How near is God to you? Listen for the sound of the breath in your body.

If you like the notion of breathing as a symbol of the divine presence, you may wish to use this simple exercise described by Lawrence Kushner:

Find a place and a time that are quiet enough to hear the sound of your own breathing. Simply listen to that barely audible noise and intend that with each inhalation and exhalation you sound the Name of Being. It may be no accident that this exercise is universally acknowledged as an easy and effective method for focusing and relaxation.

Just before we leave this idea of breathing and pronouncing the unpronounceable Name of God, it is fascinating to note also Rabbi Kushner's translation of the sound that Elijah heard after the great wind, the earthquake and the fire (1 Kings 19:11–13). Violent, awe-inspiring phenomena, often associated with prophetic utterances, this time carried no word from God. Then came a noise which Rabbi Kushner says is virtually untranslatable for it is something like a 'small sound of thin silence'. Our modern translations, as ever, attempt to demystify the moment with bland renderings, 'a gentle whisper' (NIV), 'a faint, murmuring sound' (REB). In fact the old AV is probably nearer the mark with its strangely evocative 'still small voice'. Lawrence Kushner translates the phrase as 'the soft, barely audible sound of almost breathing'. God's word to Elijah sounded like the man's own breathing, a thought which moves our reflection forward to meditative prayer.

Meditation is focused contemplation

In the biblical tradition, meditation is active, purposeful contemplation, with the mind applied to the subject of meditation. People who are meditating will be on their guard against distractions, ready to expel discordant thoughts or images. Meditation is not a dreamy mystical reverie but the searching work of an encounter with God.

Meditative prayer arises when a word of God is received from the surface of the mind into the reflective mind where it is allowed to yield its light and wisdom. The Lord appears within his word, initiating a conversation which is unhurried, even leisurely, but definite. It extends into habitual awareness of the Lord as that word thrives in our deepest mind, drawing out our response in prayer. As a consequence, the interior climate is altered. As with physical climate change, so too our interior 'landscape' is affected, the desert is reclaimed and made fertile, and new plantings of the Holy Spirit flourish.

Meditation is described in various ways: it is sometimes compared to *sucking a cough sweet*, something we do without consciously thinking about it; we simply put it in the mouth and trust it to do its soothing work. We also speak of *mulling over* a verse or an idea; or we *ponder* it as we allow the verse to move in the imagination, and to *percolate* through our thinking, colouring whatever it touches. We may also compare the meditative process to *pebbles* on the beach.

Refining the stones

Pebbles on the beach are smoothed and rounded through unknown years of rubbing against sand and other stones under the action of the sea. If we compare the pebbles to our thoughts, they are turned over and over, shaped and polished within the 'sand and sea' of God's word in the mind. God's thoughts towards us are compared to sand:

> How precious to me are your thoughts, O God!
>   How vast is the sum of them!
> Were I to count them,
>   They would outnumber the grains of sand . . .
>
> Psalm 139:17,18

In meditation, God's thoughts interact with our thinking like the process whereby rough, unremarkable pebbles are transformed into lovely and original things.

That process is mimicked in the jeweller's workshop when semi-precious stones or pebbles are placed in a drum with a fine polishing paste. The motor-driven drum is switched on and left to trundle around for hours, or even days, as gradually the stones are smoothed and polished by the action until they become attractive enough to use in jewellery or ornamentation. In this analogy, the stones are our thoughts, the polishing paste is the words of our meditation, and the rotating drum which causes the polishing action may be compared to the process of meditation. From time to time the jeweller will stop the drum to inspect the progress among his pebbles. Similarly, within our meditation it is interesting to pause and observe the way our thoughts are changing as they are shaped and refined over time.

For further direction on meditative prayer, we now turn to those masters of the art, the psalmists. They are fascinating teachers.

'The soul is dyed the colour of its leisure thought'

Our lives have huge diversity and variety in them, but they lack unity because they don't have a centre around which to gather. The lives of the people we call the psalmists, who lived some 2,500 years ago, may strike us as unbearably lacking in variety, but they had a unity and their meditations and prayers show how they worked at strengthening that unity by gathering everything around the centre – which was God.

We may not envy the psalmists their standard of living, preferring our cars to their camels, our hospitals to their medicinal herbs. But we can only envy their clarity of spiritual vision and the way they centre their lives on God. Their delight in God kept them meditating and praying when on guard duty through the night:

> My eyes stay open through the watches of the night,
>   that I may meditate on your promises.
>
> Psalm 119:148

> On my bed I remember you;
>   I think of you through the watches of the night.
>
> Psalm 63:6

> At midnight I rise to give you thanks
>   for your righteous laws.
>
> Psalm 119:62

We shouldn't think of those old believers as locked into an inflexible regime of prayer. Rather it is clear that they couldn't wait to come before the Lord for they couldn't get enough of his presence; they were motivated by desire, not duty:

> O God, you are my God,
>   earnestly I seek you;
> my soul thirsts for you,
>   my body longs for you,
> in a dry and weary land
>   where there is no water.
>
> Psalm 63:1

Thirsting for him, longing for him, clinging to him for dear life, leaning against him, quietly weaned like a child (Psalm 131); fixing their gaze on God like a servant anxious to please (Psalm

140

123:2); delighted to acknowledge their need of grace (Psalm 51:7), completely satisfied with the imperishability of God's love (Psalm 103:15–18). A typical phrase is 'My heart is steadfast, O God' (Psalm 57:7; 'fixed' in the AV).

A murmuring spring

The psalmists lived by meditation on God's mighty acts, in a continuous flow of remembering, repeating, reflecting, praying, praising and singing.

> I *remember* the days of long ago;
> I *meditate* on all your works
> and *consider* what your hands have done.
>
> Psalm 143:5

In biblical meditation we resist amnesia, our careless forgetting of the past, and we learn to recall before the face of God his marvellous deeds in creation, providential love and salvation. 'Remember the days of old' (Deuteronomy 32:7) is not a call to retreat into a comforting nostalgia for 'the good old days', but a saving reminder that what God has already done holds the key to what he is doing now and will do in the future. He has already taken the destiny of the world into his hands.

In his prayer for the churches, Paul asks for them the immense blessing of a powerful recollection of what God has already achieved in Christ: '. . . to grasp how wide and long and high and deep is the love of Christ, and to know this love that surpasses knowledge – that you may be filled to the measure of all the fulness of God' (Ephesians 3:18,19). Like a nuclear detonation two thousand years ago, the love of Christ radiates out in all directions, energising our present and future life. 'Remember, consider, meditate' on Christ's crucified love, because the more carefully and habitually we reflect on the incarnation, the cross, the resurrection and the outpoured Holy Spirit, the more hopefully we will face the future. To our impatient plea that the Lord

141

will give his people 'a new word' the psalmists and apostles raise the question 'what have you done with his earlier word?'

The meditative psalmists experienced the word of the Lord like a continuously murmuring spring of water flowing in the heart and the mouth.

> Blessed are those . . .
> [whose] delight is in the law of the LORD
>   and on his law they meditate day and night.
>
> Psalm 1:1,2

This suggests a dialogue of mutual blessing. Recalling and reflecting on God's word brings blessings for us, and in response we bless (thank) the Lord for all his marvellous acts. When the well dried up in our house in Thailand on one occasion, we called for the man who knew how to release the water again. He climbed down to the bottom of the well and worked at clearing the accumulation of rubble covering the 'eye' of the well, until the spring was able to bubble up once again and fill the well. What can we do to release the murmuring spring of meditative prayer within ourselves, or is that exclusively the ministry of the Holy Spirit?

'I have hidden your word in my heart' (Psalm 119:11)

To do this is *our* work. If we will not exert ourselves to bring the word from the surface of the mind down into the deeper reflective mind ('the heart'), it will not of itself happen. What will happen, as Jesus warns in his parable of the seed, the soil and the harvest (Matthew 13:1–9,18–23), is that any word we hold only superficially will vanish. But the word which is received into the reflective heart (the old formula was 'read, mark, learn and inwardly digest') flows like a stream throughout the inner world of thought, imagination and will, and the Lord appears in the midst of his word. Thus inner dialogue occurs when we receive the-Lord-in-his-word by remembering, repeating, reflecting, praying, obeying. Too easily we tire and stop short of that rich encounter with him. Urs Balthasar comments:

142

What manners! To receive God's daily visit not in the living room of one's soul but in the kitchen or in the hallway![5]

In the heart and by heart

Saints skilled at conversing with the Lord in the meditative mind urge that we go the next step and have the word not only *in* the heart but also *by* heart. 'What is known by heart, the heart knows' was a rabbinical principle, grounded in the wisdom of the Old Testament. When Deuteronomy charges, 'These commandments that I give you today are to be upon your hearts' (Deuteronomy 6:6), it means that the reader or listener should 'remain conscious' of them. In similarly striking terms, we are required to take the words of wisdom and,

Bind them on your fingers; write them on the tablet of your heart.

Proverbs 7:3

We are to keep them steadily present in the mind by committing them to memory. When Jeremiah says about the people's sin that it is 'engraved with an iron tool, inscribed with a flint point, on the tablets of their hearts' (Jeremiah 17:1), it means that the heart has become the memory; its awareness cannot be erased; the heart is a permanent reminder. Paul writes similarly to the Corinthian Christians:

You yourselves are our letter, written on our hearts, known and read by everybody. You show that you are a letter from Christ . . . written not with ink but with the Spirit of the living God . . . on tablets of human hearts.

2 Corinthians 3:2,3

The heart is the place of knowledge and memory. The neuroscientist Steven Rose writes of memory that it 'defines who we are and shapes the way we act more closely than any other single aspect of our personhood',[6] which suggests that we have it within our power to effect the shaping of our actions, and indeed our own personhood, by imprinting into the texture of our memory the wisdom of God's life-giving word. George Steiner writes on the power of the memorised words:

> To learn by heart is to afford the text an indwelling clarity and life-force . . . What we know by heart becomes an agency in our consciousness, a 'pace-maker' in the growth of the vital complication of our identity . . . Accurate remembrance not only deepens our grasp of the text; it generates a shaping reciprocity between ourselves and that which the heart knows.[7]

Memory nourishes prayer

Notice, once again, the order of things: first we receive God's word deeply into our hearts so that we are conscious of its presence running through our inner life like a subterranean stream; listen carefully and you will be able to hear it murmuring within you. We can express our gratitude to the Lord for the gracious activity of his word within us by memorising those parts of it that come to us with particular significance and urgency.

Thus we are empowered and advised by our heart-memory for meditative prayer. Our thoughts on the words of Scripture are shaped, enlarged and refined as they work upon each other in the 'polishing drum' of meditation. Notice how over time your thoughts become original insights into the meaning of God's word, and those insights seep into your imagination and behaviour.

The evil one will not allow this transformative process to go unchallenged. Expect him to attempt to subvert your concentration and to induce amnesia. His purpose is to create a sustained forgetting of Christian memories so that we lose the vital sense of the Lord's presence within his word within the heart, which is the memory.

Keep the word to give it away

The blessing of a heart murmuring with meditative prayer, inspired by the word of God written on the walls of the memory, is not exclusively for ourselves. In the biblical tradition it becomes the way in which the word of God is transmitted to others:

> One generation will commend your works to another;
> they will tell of your mighty acts.
> They will speak of the glorious splendour of your majesty,
> and I will meditate on your wonderful works.
>
> Psalm 145:4,5

> Hear, O Israel . . . These commandments that I give you today are to be upon your hearts [ie in your memory]. Impress them on your children . . .
>
> Deuteronomy 6:4–7

Dominic in the thirteenth century believed that the purpose of receiving the word of God through remembering-repeating-reflecting-praying-obeying was 'to contemplate, and pass on to others the things contemplated'.

A picture emerges from these remarks, and from the scriptures we have quoted, of people making God's word their own as they receive it with prayerful meditation. Their understanding of the Lord's wisdom spills out, not in a preachy manner, but as the overspill of word and prayer murmuring in their heart. They are a thoughtful people, who delight in God and his gifts in the world. They cultivate a rich imaginative thought-life. They guard the door to the soul:

> . . . whatever is true, whatever is noble, whatever is right, whatever is pure, whatever is lovely, whatever is admirable – if anything is excellent or praiseworthy – think about such things.
>
> Philippians 4:8

145

Questions for reflection and discussion

1. Glance through the chapter once again and list the various metaphors and images for 'meditation on the word in the heart'. Which ones do you find most helpful? Now coin your own metaphors.

2. From the various scriptures quoted in this chapter take a verse and follow the psalmist by 'remembering, repeating, reflecting, praying, obeying'. Or, put another way, place the verse in the 'polishing drum' of your meditative mind, and see what happens (p 139).

3. We have noted some of the remarkable properties of God's word stored in the memory. For instance, 'It extends into habitual awareness of the Lord as that word thrives in our deepest mind, drawing out our response in prayer' (p 138). And again, 'We are empowered and advised by our heart-memory for meditative prayer' (p 144). Discuss the psalmist's claim that 'even at night my heart instructs me' (Psalm 16:7). Is he suggesting that the heart 'plays back its memorised word'? Even while we sleep?

4. With other Christians, consider the place of contemplation in faith-sharing: 'To contemplate and pass on to others the things contemplated' (p 145).

Chapter 15

WHEN GOD IS SILENT

'He didn't actually accuse God of inefficiency, but when he prayed his tone was loud and angry, like that of a dissatisfied guest in a carelessly managed hotel.'[1]

It could be worse, as when a friend is quietly disappointed with prayer. 'I prayed and prayed; for years I've prayed about that difficulty but nothing happens'. We feel embarrassed on the prayer's behalf, or rather on God's behalf. What can we say? Can we suggest to our friend that when prayer makes no discernable difference God has his 'plan B'? But it is clear from Jesus' most emphatic prayer-parable about the persistent widow that there is no plan B. Don't stop in the face of apparently unanswered prayer: pray straight on through the mystery of God's silence. Jesus offers no alternative to sustained importunity in prayer.

> Then Jesus told his disciples a parable to show them that they should always pray and not give up. He said: 'In a certain town there was a judge who neither feared God nor cared about people. And there was a widow in that town who kept coming to him with the plea, "Grant me justice against my adversary."
>
> For some time he refused. But finally he said to himself, "Even though I don't fear God or care about people, yet because this widow keeps bothering me, I will see that she gets justice, so that she won't eventually wear me out with her coming!"'
>
> And the Lord said, 'Listen to what the unjust judge says. And will not God bring about justice for his chosen ones, who cry out to him day and night? Will he keep putting them off? I tell you, he will see

that they get justice, and quickly. However, when the Son of Man comes, will he find faith on the earth?'

Luke 18:1–8

We are asked to imagine a daunting human situation – a defenceless, vulnerable widow against a lazy, corrupt magistrate who hasn't a shred of mercy in his body. With no influential friends to speak for her, and too poor to offer bribes, either she rolls over and accepts her fate or she resorts to the one weapon left to her – she will nag this man into submission. He gives in 'so that she won't wear me out with her coming!' (v 5). Another translation gives 'lest she end by scratching my eyes out'.[2]

The point of the parable is that when faced with silence we 'should always pray and not give up' (v 1). What is it we shouldn't 'give up'? Don't give up praying, obviously; but in the case of the persistent widow it was her life which she refused to give up. She pleaded endlessly to survive: her very existence was at stake. We may paraphrase as follows: 'Jesus showed his disciples that they should always pray and not give up *the life that God had set them to live.*'

Notice, incidentally, that the text doesn't say 'we should always pray and not work.' Yet many of us are inclined to set prayer over and against effort as though we must choose between two alternative ways of responding to life's demands – either we take the 'spiritual' line and bring them to prayer, or we get up off our knees and do something about those problems ourselves. Clearly, Jesus wouldn't recognise such a separation between the spiritual and the practical response. He connects persistent prayer to equally persistent action. Perhaps your own efforts will be one means by which God answers your prayers.

No passive prayer

'No surrender' applies to the totality of our calling to Christian discipleship. It is an all-consuming commitment for which 'always pray' is the essential fuel. In Jesus' understanding, prayer was not an alternative to action but its inseparable twin: wherever one goes the other must also. The sort of prayer he calls us to, prayer like 'the persistent widow', rejects passivity, inaction and acquiescence in the face of delayed answers. In terms of Nehemiah's classic demonstration of prayer allied to effort when rebuilding the walls of Jerusalem in the face of a dangerous enemy, '. . . we prayed to our God and posted a guard day and night to meet this threat' (Nehemiah 4:9). They worked with trowel and spear (4:16–18), symbolic of hard work and the prayer of faith. It is the kind of prayer that rebels against plans and actions that clearly dishonour God, in society or in the church. It has been pointed out that almost everything said in the New Testament regarding prayer is not in order to reconcile us to things as they are, but to change things.

Reflect for a moment on the quality of prayer life in purposeful congregations. Isn't it the case that there appears to be a vital connection between what those congregations do in their various ministries and the energy of their prayers? Those who are engaged in 'cutting-edge' ministries (a cliché, but a good one!) seem to have an urgency and a liveliness to their prayer and worship as though the mental, spiritual and indeed the physical energy consumed by their works makes prayer for them a life-necessity, an essential source of energy and inspiration.

One such congregation in Leicester is committed to a number of exciting initiatives, including fashioning a relevant form of witness to the Islamic population. When their architect reported that the church building was severely infiltrated with dry rot, the congregation responded by refusing to accept the obvious corollary of the report, the severe curtailment of their life and ministry. Instead, they prayed. Make of this what you will, but when the architect looked again at the building, to his astonishment the dry rot was no longer active. Churches who work hard to fulfil their calling as 'light, seed, yeast, salt' are the hard-praying ones. Conversely, perhaps the reason why prayer in some churches feels thin and ineffectual is that their people are not engaged in vigorous effort for the kingdom of God locally. Hence the farcical spectacle of Christians who pray regularly for mission on the far side of the world yet who wouldn't cross the road to share the gospel with a near neighbour. Importunate, persistent prayer accompanies the hard work of practical obedience to the Lord. John Baillie comments that 'prayer unaccompanied by hard work, and work unaccompanied by urgent prayer are two things that Jesus Christ not only never preached but never even contemplated as a plausible possibility.'[3]

The grace of persistence

The widow of Jesus' parable stuck to her strategy of hounding the judge into action because, frankly, she had nowhere else to go; no other route was open to her; either she persuaded this man or she was finished. We will emulate her, untiring tenacity in our praying, but for the quite opposite reason that our God is not a merciless oriental despot but the all-loving 'Abba Father' who calls upon us to 'Ask . . . seek . . . knock' and promises that we shall 'receive . . . find . . . the door will be opened' (Matthew 7:7,8). So, not the shrill insistence of a desperate Semitic widow, but the requests of confident children to their boundlessly generous Father. Why then the apparent silence from heaven? We cannot but speculate on why persistence is necessary.

Look at the conclusion of the parable: Jesus is saying that we need have no doubts concerning God's commitment to his children's requests. 'And will not God bring about justice for his chosen ones, who cry out to him day and night . . . he will see that they get justice . . .' (Luke 18:7,8). Then comes the punchline, as Jesus repositions the question, turning the tables on his doubting followers as if to say, 'Don't you worry about God's part – have no doubts on that score – but the real question is "When the Son of Man comes, will he find faith on earth?"' (v 8). That is, will he find the church 'always praying and not giving up' on our witness to the world?

What is the sign of vital faith? Is it that we continue to pray because when we do, like pushing the correct buttons on an ATM cash dispenser, blessings pop out? That would prove nothing more than that we know how to win the Lottery. Rather, the faith that our Lord Jesus hopes to find, but doubts that he will, is knitted out of tougher material; it doesn't give up. It is a faith that seeks God as a compass needle seeks magnetic north. It says, 'I will always go to the Father because fullness of life is in him.' A faith that interprets the mystery of God's ways, not least his apparent silence, by the absolute certainty of his love for us. As Paul's famous logic has it, 'He who did not spare his own Son, but gave him up for us all – how will he not also, along with him, graciously give us all things?' (Romans 8:32).

Clearly, certain things concerning our relationship with God the Trinity are so precious that he desires to draw them out in us, testing them in the crucible of experience to show if the faith we profess in is the real thing. The persistent widow, waiting outside the judge's front door, was most certainly genuine in her relentless pursuit of justice. In a word, 'she meant it.' It is as though the Father is saying to us when we come in prayer, 'Yes, but do you mean it? Show me how much you mean it. Do you mean it enough to "always pray without giving up?"'

Isn't it worth having our faith tested even by what might be bewildering and desperate situations, so that it 'may be proved genuine and may result in praise, glory and honour when Jesus Christ is revealed'? (1 Peter 1:7). No one in his right mind will go looking for such testings, but God reserves the right to choose them for his children as his wisdom and fatherly love advise. Many could point to profoundly enriching experiences in dark times, more than in sunny times. Thus George Herbert describes a desperate experience as though he were a mountaineer pressed up against a rock on the north face of the Eiger, hanging on, just, by his fingertips:

> Only my soul hangs on to thy promises
> with face and hands clinging to thy breast,

> clinging and crying, crying without cease,
> Thou art my rock, thou art my rest.[4]

There speaks one who 'always prays', refusing to 'give up', and comes away with priceless things.

Discoveries within 'silence'

There is more going on in God's response to our prayers than meets the eye. In his love for us, our Abba Father makes prayer into a school, or schooling. Far from being a sign of aloof indifference to our requests, God's apparent silences (we must always qualify 'silence' with 'apparent') refine our faith, test the sincerity of our love for him, and attune our faculties of spiritual perception so that we learn to listen more closely to the silence. The Christian should listen for him, 'with the ear of a wild Arab listening in a silent desert', said Coleridge,[5] since who knows what God is saying in apparent silences.

Yet once again our thinking turns back to Elijah's mysterious experience of God's silence following the tremendous, but empty, noise of the great wind, shattering rocks, earthquake and fire (1 Kings 19:11,12). God was silent within the noise. At that point, when the great prophetic phenomena had yielded no word from God, Elijah may have felt inclined to pack up and move on. It is a sign of his greatness that he stayed attentive 'with the ear of a wild Arab listening in a silent desert' until he heard the voice of God speaking with 'the soft, barely audible sound of almost breathing'. It was an advanced class in 'prayer as schooling'.

Spiritually perceptive people urge us to humble our minds and listen to the silence. One goes so far as to say that 'silence is the language God speaks and everything else is a bad translation.'[6] Being a wordy, noisy soul, I struggle rather with that sort of comment. After all, Christ is the Word, not the Silence. But those wise people are simply sending to the rest of us messages of reassurance and encouragement, 'The silence isn't empty – it isn't even silent

– the Lord is saying, "be still and know that I am God" (Psalm 46:10).' If this is so, the silence of apparently unanswered prayer is an invitation to come and stand closer to the speaker, learn to listen for the voice which may be no louder than the sound of your own breathing.

While thinking along these lines, I came across an amazing report regarding powers of perception and intuition. It was headed 'Blind man can see emotions in others'. The article described tests done at the University of Wales in Bangor by a team of neuroscientists with a fifty-two year old man who had lost his sight after two successive strokes had destroyed his visual cortices, the link between his eyes and the part of the brain involved in vision. The man could see nothing. His world was dark and he could not distinguish movement, colours, shapes, or even the presence of bright light. The article went on to explain that the part of the brain involved in recognising emotion in the faces of others is the amygdala, a region quite distinct from the part involved in normal vision. The team wanted to know if this completely blind man could recognise the emotions of fear, anger and happiness in pictures of faces, ie if the amygdala could 'see' without using normal vision.

They showed the man 200 pictures of people's faces, showing a range of emotions. He got them right almost 60 per cent of the time, a rate significantly higher than chance. For myself, that jaw-dropping disclosure causes me to think again about what our spiritual antennae might pick up within silence.

Creative untidiness

In the process of waiting on God, unusual things may happen. It is as though the mind of God, his will for our life, were written in the form of a music score. Music has the mystical powers both to hold the performer, the musician or singer, under its discipline while at the same time releasing her to read, interpret and play the piece to the utmost limits of her gifts and inventiveness. A beginner must stay strictly within the given score, while the accomplished player is free to interpret with all the flair she can. She can 'see' and 'hear' within the given music possibilities not written down. The written score points her in the right direction; the rest is up to her.

Something similar seems to be happening with us when we open up our life to God in prayer. If you like, a prayerful reading of life has the character of a musician interpreting music, or of a child playing a game. God points us in the right direction, he provides the clues, but then we must go with it and follow it to who knows where. This is possible only if God allows us room by not giving us all the answers. His silence makes the 'game', or our interpretations and performance of the music, possible. Or would you rather he told you everything now?

> I went to the theatre
> With the author of a successful play.
> He insisted on explaining everything;
> Told me what to watch;
> The details of directions,
> The errors of the property man,
> The foibles of the star.
> He anticipated all my surprises
> And ruined the evening.
> Never again! And mark you,
> The greatest author of all
> Made no such mistake.[7]

This meditation is taking us in interesting directions. From the mystery of apparently unanswered prayer, to the blessings which can come to us out of the Father's silence; then the question of our being attuned to however he chooses to speak to us, even in silence, and the freedom by which silence allows us to grow as we experiment with reading God's will for our lives. Taken together, those thoughts question the wisdom of our tendency to look for spiritual neatness and tidiness. To such minds, God's silence is frustrating since it cannot be made to fit clear patterns in which everyone, including God, knows his part and performs it. Consider this old newspaper cutting:

> In recent years the magnificent pine trees in Kensington Park . . . have been dying. Experts say there can be little doubt that this is due to the misdirected tidiness of the gardeners who swept up the old dead pine needles and left the roots without natural comfort and protection.

A certain amount of chaos, loose ends, and parts that seem not to fit together, is probably a healthy sign that God is at work and needs a little more time to finish. His silences are part of his creative untidiness in our prayer lives.

A people of possibility

Tidiness – that was the disciples' view of Christ's mission. The way they liked everything in its place and functioning as it should was a clue to their spiritual insecurity in their new job as disciples. Then along comes a maverick interloper who breaks the rules in her determination to get through to Jesus. Another wonderful woman, also in desperate need (Matthew 15:21–28), she enacts everything we have been saying about the Lord's silence in response to our prayer and the scope that silence affords for our own imagination to thrive.

The Canaanite woman saw in Jesus' presence possibilities for her 'demon-possessed' daughter's healing. 'Lord, Son of David, have mercy on me!' (v 22). But he fends her off by naming the established theological orthodoxy: 'I was sent only to the lost sheep of Israel' (v 24). Worse than silence, this reply seems to be cruel. In fact he is probing her seriousness: he wants to know whether or not she means it when she credits him with the titles, 'Lord, Son of David'. He draws her out, urging her to look at the potential of the present moment and imagine how it might be transformed. Does she see? Can she visualise new possibilities for her daughter?

This encounter takes on the character of a game – the woman makes her move, and Jesus blocks it and waits for her next move. (Is this chess? or football?). She leaves the disciples gasping as she challenges convention and attacks Jesus on his most vulnerable point, his compassion, with her heart-breaking cry, 'Lord, help me' (v 25). He counters and tries to catch her in his offside trap. 'It is not right to take the children's bread and toss it to their dogs.' But the woman has glimpsed healing for her daughter; she slips past his offside ploy and advances to score the winning goal with wonderful audacity. 'Yes, Lord . . . but even the dogs eat the crumbs that fall from their masters' table' (v 27). Jesus is totally delighted with the woman's faith and vision. 'You have great faith! Your request is granted.' 'And her daughter was healed from that very hour!' (v 28).

Apparently some silences are not a refusal but an invitation that we look again, and this time with imaginative faith; then tell the Lord what it is we can see, and imagine, and what we can believe of him.

Questions for reflection and discussion

1. Look through the chapter again, listing the various interpretations of God's silence when we pray. Which of them speaks most clearly to your own experience? 'In the process of waiting on God, unusual things may happen' (p 153). Share with your group some of the 'unusual things'.
2. Jesus 'connects persistent prayer to equally persistent action' (p 148). In those situations you are currently praying for, what 'persistent action' are you taking towards the answers to your prayers?
3. 'A wild Arab listening in a silent desert' (p 152) is an exotic image of listening to God's apparent silence – but we live in the restless cacophony of modern life. Discuss how a Christian today may realistically cultivate listening for God.
4. Jesus was fascinated by the way the Canaanite woman saw

the potential of the moment and visualised new possibilities for her daughter, even when Jesus apparently turned her down. 'Apparently some silences are not a refusal but an invitation that we look again . . . and imagine . . .' (p 156). When you apply this lesson to your own 'impossible situations' what can you see, who can you believe, what will you ask of the Lord?

Chapter 16

A CONDONED VIOLENCE

'We must not conceive of prayer as an overcoming of God's reluctance, but as a laying hold of his highest willingness'[1] – the paradox of laying hold of the God who is already on our side. We have no need to cajole him into listening, or by interminable talk to bludgeon him into granting our requests. Before it even occurs to us to turn to him he is already turned towards us, delighted to receive our approach. Yet paradoxically we are urged to come with all the focused energy of a fighter 'laying hold' of God.

This suggests an attitude very different to our customary undemanding, half-awake state of mind when we pray. 'Laying hold' of God in his 'highest willingness' has a clarity and a grip to it, convinced that vital outcomes will be decided if only we prevail with God. It is to 'lay hold' as a mountaineer lays hold of the rope, for dear life.

Many of us flinch from the intensity of this level of prayer; it seems too aggressive, imagining a struggle where there isn't any. Yet we have God's word on it that he welcomes strong, importuning prayer (eg Jesus' admiration for the two women discussed in Chapter 15). He urges, 'Ask . . . seek . . . knock . . .' (Matthew 7:7) and we have his pledge that this is not a vain endeavour but that real things will happen as a consequence.

'As a man prays, so he is'[2]

Back to the principle of first things first (see p 30), only this time the necessary knot we tie in our thread in order to sew is our confidence in God's 'highest willingness' to receive and answer prayer. Here is a test: first pray for the Holy Spirit to lead your thoughts to one of God's promises concerning the efficacy of prayer. Then, deliberately gather the burden of need or anxiety which you are carrying around with you, and place it onto the promise. If the promise is now carrying the burden you are free of it, and an awareness of lightness will be evidence that you have used the promise as Christ intended it.

However, burdens cannot always be so neatly parcelled and placed in the box marked 'promises'. We become distracted and unfocused through anxiety, which is perhaps why Paul writes, 'carry each other's burdens, and in this way you will fulfil the law of Christ' (Galatians 6:2). The writer Charles Williams covenanted with a group of Christian friends to practise the 'law of Christ' for one another. The group would share with each other the details of their burdens, how they were experienced, with what sensations of stress or dread, and at what time of day the burden became most oppressive. Thus you might covenant with a friend who is anxious about a sick child, that you will 'carry' this anxiety, in your imagination, at 3.15 in the afternoon, when the sense of burden tends to be most oppressive. You will visualise your friend's state of mind, the sense of helplessness and the dread, and open up to take the burden and carry it, transferring it onto the promise of God. The two of you will agree that if *you* are carrying it at 3.15 pm, then *your friend* must let go of the burden. You will carry it into the promises of God, acting vicariously for your friend and, in your friend's name, you leave it there.

In his novel, *Descent into Hell*,[3] Charles Williams describes a young woman, Pauline, who all her life has been stalked . . . by herself! She hears footsteps, glances back and sees herself. The experience is driving her steadily mad, until she confides in a pastor who is astonished that she hasn't entered into a covenant with a Christian friend to 'carry her burden' for her. She describes precisely the processes of the terror so that he can enter into her distress in his imagination. He advises her what to expect – 'When you hear the footsteps behind you look back. "She" will be there as usual but at that moment you will know that I am already carrying your fear, and if I've got it, you are left free with no dread to carry.'

Incidentally, with the fear lifted, and in her awareness of her strong friend carrying it instead of her, Pauline is unafraid to confront the other 'self' stalking her. It turns out to be her true self – a joyful self. 'It had been her incapacity for joy, nothing else, that had, till now, turned the vision of herself aside.'

In the interests of keeping prayer practical and real, you may like to adapt for your own use a method of intercession evolved by a youth missionary prayer group in Manchester. They would sift through reports from missionary contacts in the Far East, and display on a board a number of urgent prayer requests. The list stayed for each monthly meeting, items removed or altered only after news was received telling of movement in those situations. A second board was used at each meeting on which were highlighted fresh requests. You can see how things, and people, are kept up to the mark by that method. Incoming news is transposed into intercession and thanksgiving, and situations are followed through and not allowed to simply fade away in that inconclusive, vague manner which sucks the reality out of much of our praying. Clearly people who 'lay hold' of God in this way mean business.

Here is a second test: George MacDonald wrote 'It is the heart that is not yet sure of its God that is afraid to laugh in his presence.'[4] When we dare to 'lay hold' of God's 'highest willingness', when we are sure of his love and faithfulness, sure enough to risk our lives on his promises, the prayer becomes our secret source of joy. We are freed from the dreary need to take ourselves too seriously. Indeed, we let go of ourselves when our hands are filled with 'laying hold' of God. Here is that enviable 'inexpressible and glorious joy' which the apostle saw in his young churches (1 Peter 1:8). Laugh, sing, dance (if you must), do handstands in the street and embrace perfect strangers (if you insist) because something very wonderful has happened – we are sure of our God!

'Whoever wrestles with God in prayer puts his own life at stake'[5]

'Laying hold' is wrestler's talk. The seminal event which encourages us to think that God invites his people to wrestle with him in prayer is Jacob at the river Jabbok, when fleeing from the brother he swindled. Esau was now closing in fast with a small army.

> That night Jacob got up and took his two wives, his two female servants and his eleven sons and crossed the ford of the Jabbok. After he had sent them across the stream, he sent over all his possessions. So Jacob was left alone, and a man wrestled with him till daybreak. When the man saw that he could not overpower him, he touched the socket of Jacob's hip so that his hip was wrenched as he wrestled with the man. Then the man said, 'Let me go, for it is daybreak.'
>
> But Jacob replied, 'I will not let you go unless you bless me.'
>
> The man asked him, 'What is your name?'
>
> 'Jacob,' he answered.
>
> Then the man said, 'Your name will no longer be Jacob, but Israel, because you have struggled with both God and human beings and have overcome.'
>
> Jacob said, 'Please tell me your name.'
>
> But he replied, 'Why do you ask my name?' Then he blessed him there.
>
> So Jacob called the place Peniel, saying, 'It is because I saw God face to face, and yet my life was spared.'
>
> The sun rose above him as he passed Peniel, and he was limping because of his hip. Therefore to this day the Israelites do not eat the tendon attached to the socket of the hip, because the socket of Jacob's hip was touched near the tendon.
>
> Genesis 32:22–32

If ever a man needed divine intervention it was Jacob at the moment of 'great fear and distress' (v 7) when he was preparing to meet Esau. Yet Jacob was sure of God, sure enough to dare

161

to 'lay hold' of him by quoting the small print in every believer's relationship with God, the covenant promises – in the form he had received it. The promise was, 'I will surely make you prosper and will make your descendants like the sand of the sea, which cannot be counted' (v 12). The contrast between Jacob's actual situation and the immensities of the covenant promise is almost comic, but that's the nature of faith. Earlier at Bethel (28:1–19) God had reaffirmed his covenant commitment to Jacob (and through Jacob to the whole human family) in the awesome ladder dream, 'I am with you and will watch over you wherever you go . . . I will not leave you until I have done what I have promised you' (28:15). How a man in a tight corner can use a promise to lay hold of God is memorably demonstrated in what happened next: 'So Jacob was left alone, and a man wrestled with him till daybreak' (32:24). The 'man' was a theophany, God incognito, God-as-that-man, for next day Jacob named the place Peniel, meaning 'I saw God face to face.'

Promises that Jacob knew in his head, and by heart, were here incarnated in this gasping, panting stranger as the two crashed around in the river. Jacob 'laid hold' of God, and God allowed himself to be wrestled into submission in that rough, tough, desperate scrap. Why did God make Jacob wrestle for his blessing? Was it to purge him of his deceitfulness and cunning, his tendency to put on an act and distort his relationships? Was it in order to make the point to Jacob and his descendants, down to the church and ourselves, that God's covenant promises require to be claimed with every fibre of our being? Was God setting Jacob certain searching questions in that fight, 'You say you depend on me, that you trust me, but do you mean it? Show me!' That contest was not decided by Jacob talking God into submission (like the persistent widow) but by his unshakeable tenacity in 'laying hold' of God (like the Canaanite woman). Jesus says that we best bear witness to the Father's providential love by the brevity and simplicity of our prayers (Matthew 6:7). It is not in the saying of words, or even in the words we say, so much as by a heart set on holding God to his promises: 'I will not let you go unless you bless me' (32:26).

How physical is spiritual? Are we right to spiritualise the Jabbok fight completely? Doesn't our body language have a place within sincere, earnest prayer? We are not pure spirit: we are bodily spirits, or spiritual bodies, and our hearts' desires express themselves at least partially through the body; the physical expression of our spiritual tenacity is all part of our engagement with God. Consider this observation from Jewish spirituality: 'Glorify the Lord, and exalt him as much as you can, for he surpasses even that. When you exalt him, summon all your strength, and do not grow weary, for you cannot praise him enough. Who has seen him and can describe him? Or who can extol him as he is?'[6] The writer suggests that sincere worshippers are engaged in something of a contest in which they strive to keep up with the runaway beauty of God.

Threats, anarchy, violence

God invites us to wrestle with him for our blessing! He welcomes our assault, he condones violence in prayer when we 'lay hold' of him knowing his 'highest willingness' to bless us. He opens himself to our prayer as importunity. At this point we need a little help from some of the great ones experienced in 'anarchy and violence', and gifted in explaining that level of prayer to the rest of us.

John Donne (1572–1631) said this about wrestling with God:

Earnest prayer has the nature of importunity ... we press, we importune God ... Prayer has the nature of impudence; we threaten God in prayer ... and God suffers this impudence and more. Prayer has the nature of violence; in the public prayers of the congregation, we besiege God, says Tertullian, and we take God prisoner, and bring God to our conditions, and God is glad to be straightened by us in that siege.[7]

John Donne – poet, preacher, soldier – had a violent and bloody initiation into warfare in an English naval attack which destroyed a Spanish fleet in Cadiz harbour in 1597 and razed the city and its castle and fortifications. Perhaps those violent memories seeped into Donne's understanding of spiritual warfare, but the onslaught is directed at God!

As a friend of the Herbert family Donne may have related his war experiences to the young George Herbert, whose own metaphors for importunate prayer are startling. From his great sonnet 'Prayer' (p 135,136) we will look at three images.

Prayer is 'Engine against the Almighty'

The 'engine' is the old military engineer's construction for assaulting enemy fortifications, to lay siege, batter walls, tunnel under defences and blow open doors. We are familiar with the idea of prayer as a weapon 'against the powers of this dark world and against the spiritual forces of evil in the heavenly realms. Therefore . . . pray in the Spirit on all occasions with all kinds of prayers and requests. . . .' (Ephesians 6:12,18). But Herbert is suggesting something very different when he turns the assault engine against the Lord himself! And not against God as the amiable Father but as 'the Almighty'!

The poet extends the logic of God's promise – '. . . I tell you the truth, my Father will give you whatever you ask in my name' (John 16:23) – which puts authority and power into the hands of God's people praying in the world. We have his siege-engine and the assurance that no power on earth can withstand prayer in Christ's name. On earth or *heaven.* Herbert pictures a white flag hoisted over heaven's gates and the Lord himself emerging, arms raised in surrender, ready to grant our demands. If that hair-raising talk smacks of an over-heated imagination, and an over-familiarity with the holiest things, George Herbert might reasonably reply that he is simply allowing God's promises to run and run towards their full potential.

What are our demands? How ought we to handle the incredible opportunity, and responsibility, of 'Whatever you ask in my name?' Shall we emulate the schoolboy who, after a particularly stressful geography examination, prayed, 'Dear Lord, please make Copenhagen the capital of Japan, just for a few days'? But Christian prayer isn't magic, so how should we pray? Can we be trusted with such a potent 'engine'? Does common sense have any place in prayer-sense, and how can we keep personal self-ishness from our prayer? We have been here before:

1. *First tie your knot . . .* (p 30,31). Begin with the hallowing of the Father's name, his kingdom come, his will be done. Our personal requirements seem somehow to find their proper place within God-centred prayer.
2. *Remember the mother.* Even Mary seems not to have been entirely clear about her choices. She surrendered her uncer-tainties to the will of God. 'I am the Lord's servant . . . May it be to me as you have said' (Luke 1:38), she prayed. Could there be a more powerful request?
3. *Remember the Son* and the collision of his natural desire for self-preservation with the Father's will. 'My Father, if it is not possible for this cup to be taken away unless I drink it, may your will be done' (Matthew 26:42).
4. *Remember that God's plans for us are 'what perfect wisdom suggests to infinite love'.*[8] Nothing we suggest or request in prayer can exceed in wisdom the Father's 'good, pleasing and perfect will' (Romans 12:2). The most powerful use we can make of prayer, the 'engine against the Almighty', is to plead for our lives to proceed within his plans, and then go cheerfully on our way knowing that 'My Father will give you whatever you ask in my name.'

Praying for healing

'I prayed so much for my mother when she fell ill with cancer. Friends at church prayed for her, she was even prayed for in Sunday services, for months. But nothing happened. She died.'

How often we have heard similar accounts of apparently futile prayer, made even more painful, if that were possible, by different stories of wonderful healing and recovery. Where is the 'engine against the Almighty' when loved ones are ill?

The most helpful approach to 'prayer for healing' I've encountered recently was at the Community of the Holy Name in Derby. Sister Lilias is herself confined to a wheelchair yet conducts a remarkable prayer-ministry for the sick who come in to her regular meetings. At each gathering she explains that God could answer prayer in any of four ways.

1. He can, and he will, heal you tonight;
2. or he may say 'I will heal you but later. There are things going on in your life that must be dealt with first';
3. or his answer to you may be, 'My grace is sufficient for you';
4. or he may tell you, 'I'm preparing you for death.'
   (Sister Lilias commented on the remarkable interest people show in this fourth possibility, as if it is a liberation to be allowed 'officially' to embrace the possibility of death.)

Prayer is 'Reversed Thunder'

George Herbert's next image is as audacious as the 'engine'. Normally thunder is top down, from heaven to us, without warning or waiting for permission. Thunder happens to us, we are thundered at and upon. Herbert is suggesting that what thunder does to us on earth, our prayers do to God's heaven. Like thunder, prayer cannot be withstood. In Jesus' estimation to be equipped with prayer is enough, that and the Holy Spirit – or, more exactly, prayer *in* the Holy Spirit. The Lord left us with little else in this world other than 'My Father will give you whatever you ask in my name.'

Thunder from heaven rattles the teacups on earth, loosening slates on the roof and terrifying large dogs and small children. Thunder is a spooky, goose-bump-raising moment that puts us in our place, feeling fragile, vulnerable and threatened. It is the cosmic butler's tap on the shoulder to draw our attention to the fact that we are not as invincible as we imagine ourselves to be. It is awesome. Isn't it odd, therefore, to suggest an analogy between thunder and prayer? Rather, the two seem completely opposite to each other, thunder being everything prayer isn't. A terrific din that no one can ignore, contrasting with the soft murmur of voices at prayer behind closed doors which everyone can ignore. But Herbert is suggesting that prayer storms into heaven with all the unstoppable authority of thunder storming at us on earth. Prayer in Christ's name, the irresistible power of the prayer of love, love-at-prayer, prayer because of love. Heaven is delighted to be shaken by the 'reversed thunder' of such prayer.

Finally, we shall look at a third image of violence in Herbert's prayer sonnet.

Prayer is 'Christ-side-piercing spear'

Christians of all traditions will agree that vital prayer reaches into the heart of God, into the heart of Christ. The first person to do that wasn't a mystic or an apostle but a Roman soldier in the execution squad. Whether for reasons of mercy or casual brutality, he 'pierced Jesus' side with a spear, bringing a sudden flow of blood and water' (John 19:34). The outflow of blood and water was the outflow of Jesus' life. With tremendous imaginative power George Herbert sees our prayers reaching into Jesus, releasing the saving outflow of his inexhaustible life, as that spear penetrated deep into his body. Among the worshippers whose practice was to contemplate the wounds of Christ (see p 127,128), the spear wound in the side was reckoned most precious because it opened a way into the heart of Jesus where he bears the burdens of his people. And it says, in the most stark form imaginable, that our Lord Jesus took flesh like his people.

This astounding metaphor holds marvellous significance for our praying. First, it responds to a deep-seated anxiety which casts a shadow across our communion with God and our joy and confidence in prayer. It is the fact that we are people of flesh trying to stay in communion with God who 'lives in unapproachable light' (1 Timothy 6:16). The gospel reveals that in Christ God comes to us from out of his 'unapproachable light', crossing the divine-human abyss to enter our human nature, in our flesh.

We touch God in prayer, not on the side of his 'unapproachable light' but in his flesh, which is our flesh. We touch God in 'the flesh of God' when our prayers enter like a spear thrust through Christ's open side into his heart. The 'flesh of God' is our touching-place. He said at the resurrection, '. . . Touch me and see; a ghost does not have flesh and bones, as you see I have' (Luke 24:39).

Consider the Christ-life which flows out in response to the spear-thrust of our prayers, from the heart of him 'who has been tempted in every way, just as we are – yet was without sin'. (Hebrews 4:15). In Jesus, God became an 'insider' with us in the full realities of our human experience. For your meditation, reflect on these astonishing words from an ancient Ascension Day hymn:

> The flesh offends, the flesh atones;
> The flesh of God now reigns as God.[9]

Look again at chapter 10, 'The Insider'.

Questions for reflection and discussion

1. Have you ever seriously attempted to 'carry each other's burdens' in a prayer-covenant (p 159)? Something like Charles Williams' method could have a transforming effect on Christian fellowship. Discuss the possibilities with your friends.
2. Praying through to a conclusion (p 160). Would you consider adapting the 'Manchester' model for your own church or prayer-group practice?

3. 'Laying hold of God – threats, anarchy, violence'. Do you agree that 'many of us flinch from the intensity of this level of prayer . . . (p 158)? What do you make of George Herbert's three pictures of prayer as siege engine, reversed thunder and the spear? Discuss the suggestion that at heart many of us dare not think of wrestling with God in prayer because we are not sure enough of him to 'laugh in his presence' (p 160).

4. We are familiar with the idea of the believer serenely trusting the Lord for his response to our prayers, but how exactly do 'serenely trusting' people also claim God's promises 'with every fibre of our being' (p 162), like Jacob at Peniel? Perhaps it is a Jewish thing – but look again at the advice to 'put forth all your strength' in praising God: that, surely, is a Spirit-filled Christian thing.

Chapter 17

PRAYING IN BABYLON

Ten good reasons to be on your knees for the church:

1. The church is the body of Christ, who 'loved the church and gave himself up for her' (Ephesians 5:25).
2. The church is the living witness 'that God was reconciling the world to himself in Christ' (2 Corinthians 5:19).
3. By the power of the Holy Spirit the church is the agent of God's mission in the world, to 'show and tell' the gospel.
4. The church is a sign of God's 'Yes' to the world, evidence that salvation through Christ affects what happens to people in this life as well as in the next.
5. The church is also a sign of God's 'No' to claims of salvation other than by Jesus Christ (Acts 4:12).
6. The church is called to live in the tension of being, at the same time, called out of the world and sent into the world.
7. God maintains his people in the world as an 'experimental garden' (David Bosch), a display of his wisdom in the lives of men and women who are 'the firstfruits of the Spirit' (Romans 8:23).
8. Because the church lives coordinated with eternity it is a foretaste, an example and a pledge of the full reality to come (2 Corinthians 1:22).
9. The church is God's cosmic laboratory. He intends that 'through the church, the manifold wisdom of God should be made known to the rulers and authorities in the heavenly realms, according to his eternal purpose which

he accomplished in Christ Jesus our Lord' (Ephesians 3:10,11).

10. Therefore, neither a secularised church (that is, a church which concerns itself only with this-worldly activities and interests) nor a separatist church (that is, a church which involves itself only in soul-saving and preparation of converts for the hereafter) can faithfully articulate God's mission in the world.[1]

Without further comment you could use the ten points as a guide for prayer. The apostle Paul writes, 'And pray in the Spirit on all occasions with all kinds of prayers and requests. With this in mind, be alert and always keep on praying for all the saints' (Ephesians 6:18). Such prayer is always the same, in that it is 'always . . . for all the saints', yet it is oven-fresh each time because it is inwrought by the Spirit and informed by the Christian's 'alert' attention to the nature of the enemy opposed to the Lord's people.

'Alert' Christians will use Scripture as a lens through which to read, decode and interpret the challenges facing the church. That is, Scripture provides a range of analogies, events and stories which portray God's people in the world, while our part is to look prayerfully for the ones that speak most directly to our present circumstances. Do we understand ourselves best as an *Exodus people*, traversing the wilderness as quickly as possible en route to the heavenly Canaan? Or are we primarily a *conquest people*, overthrowing God's enemies as we strive to build his kingdom in the world? Or are we a *civilising*, cultivating people who not merely pass through the desert but work to cultivate it according to God's promise that 'the desert and the parched land will be glad; the wilderness will rejoice and blossom . . .' (Isaiah 35:1)? The analogy which best illustrates our circumstances will be the one best to guide our prayers 'for all the Lord's people'.

Few would deny that the church in her present condition in many Western societies is undergoing a process of death and resurrection. The old certainties have taken a tremendous pounding from the forces of modernity; we are fighting for our existence as a vital church within a confident, overbearing secularism. When we look for the biblical analogy which reflects the essence of our situation, it is surely the 'death and resurrection' event in the Old Testament, decisive for faith as for history, the exile of Israel's Babylonian captivity after the fall of Jerusalem in 587 BC. Israel's defeat and transportation north to Babylon implied God's defeat, his failure and unfaithfulness, even his absence. It seemed that an unstoppable paganism had manifestly triumphed. Israel's self-confidence, her sense of identity as the chosen people of the one true God, redeemed and appointed to serve his purposes among the nations, came under enormous strain through the captivity.

Christians, similarly, can feel outnumbered and outgunned in a culture energised by devotion to materialism's false gods, and by the sheer magnitude of apparent indifference to Christ's claims. In that mood, whether in ancient Babylon or in the present day, two responses are possible, and the impact of both on the life and the mission of our churches today is inescapable.

1. **Assimilation.** If you can't beat them, join them. Be realistic, stop fighting and go with the flow, assimilate to the dominant culture.

Some Israelites found their distinctive Jewishness too demanding and awkward to maintain: 'How can we sing the songs of the Lord while in a foreign land?' (Psalm 137:4). But if they cannot sing the Lord's songs they will soon find themselves humming along to the songs of Bel and Nebo. Similarly with Christians, the tendency is to yield to the gravitational pull of the consensus in society, and to assimilate whenever our Christian distinctiveness is too embarrassing. Hence the principle, 'Do not conform any longer to the pattern of this world, but be trans-formed by the renewing of your mind . . .' (Romans 12:2).

Pray for a Christian mind in 'all the Lord's people'. Pray that we will have the courage to wear our Christian distinctiveness with pride, to dare to be different in 'Babylon'.

2. **Despair** is a second possible response to exile, a sense that although 'Babylon' is wrong, it seems that God no longer has his

former power and authority. He has failed and we are helpless and homeless. We won't casually assimilate, but it is clear that we have lost our joy and verve, we are defensive and stoic, without vital expectation of restoration. How many in our churches maintain the framework of Christian practice, but in their hearts have long since quietly despaired of the Lord's transforming intervention?

Lord of all hope, pour your resurrection hope into our hearts, may it flood our lives, and so keep us living in daily expectation of your new work.

What is God saying to churches threatened by assimilation and despair? We return to our master analogy of Israel's Babylonian captivity.

Through the prophet Isaiah, God gave his people a number of messages in which he called upon them to make ready for God's new work in emancipation, their exit from Babylon, and return home. In Isaiah 40–55 there are at least six messages, or exercises, to prepare exiles for God's great move.[2]

1. Recover your radical memories

Assimilation and despair induce amnesia; or, if you prefer, by losing touch with our radical faith-memories, assimilation and despair have room to invade and flourish. So Isaiah calls on exiles:

> Listen to me, you who pursue righteousness
>> and who seek the LORD:
> Look to the rock from which you were cut
>> and to the quarry from which you were hewn;
> look to Abraham, your father,
>> and to Sarah, who gave you birth . . .

Isaiah 51:1,2

Get back to your origins. Remember the strange primitive story of your father and mother in the faith, Abraham and Sarah. In

173

the face of their barrenness, without hope of a child, God worked the miracle of new life. You are born out of that miracle when Abraham 'faced the fact that his body was as good as dead – since he was about a hundred years old – and that Sarah's womb was also dead' (Romans 4:19). Yet they trusted in the God of resurrection life.

Even so, the exiles shouldn't romanticise Abraham and Sarah's faith. After all, he panicked and took a surrogate wife 'just in case' God didn't come through with his miracle. And as for Sarah, remember her mocking laughter, her inability to believe and receive the promises. They were hot and cold, trusting and doubting, just like us! In spite of their failings God held to his promises and Sarah had her child.

Exiles, inclined to assimilate with Babylonian ways would like to boast of an impressive past of military and cultural achievements, the sort of history their Babylonian neighbours would admire. Isaiah won't hear of it! They must go back to those strange, primitive figures, Abraham and Sarah, as they wandered around a country not theirs, pathetically childless. Hardly the sort of founding memory to impress sophisticated Babylonians! Yet it is precisely that event of divine grace and power working for a helpless elderly couple that points the way forward. From those odd origins, miracle had entered the spiritual DNA of God's faithful people, and everything must now be interpreted in the light of this life-out-of-death God. So, make ready for new life!

That is the New Testament vision also. Our original 'birth' event is Christ crucified and risen from the dead, his people risen with him. Miracle is in our DNA also and the church cannot be understood apart from the miracle of grace in the incarnation and resurrection which are normative for Christian thinking. Assimilation marginalises the supernatural and the miraculous as an awkward embarrassment in a 'rational' culture. In order to win approval in the prevailing secularism we are tempted to articulate the faith in acceptable, reasonable and 'sophisticated' terms, and to avoid talk of salvation through a tortured Jewish manual worker – who is God. As we pray for 'all saints' we will ask for Christian minds to be utterly convinced by the gospel, seized by, grounded in, and on fire with Christ's love for us.

2. Practise radical criticism

Isaiah's next 'exercise' or 'discipline' for exiles as they prepare for God's new work is to keep an essential critical distance in relation to an impressive Babylonianism. This is both a religious and a political critique, so Isaiah ridicules Babylonian gods (what did the Babylonian police make of this assault on their culture?).

> Bel bows down, Nebo stoops low;
>> their idols are borne by beasts of burden.
> The images that are carried about are burdensome,
>> a burden for the weary.
> They stoop and bow down together;
>> unable to rescue the burden,
>> they themselves go off into captivity.
>
> Isaiah 46:1,2

The poet-prophet goes on to describe the laughable methods by which gods are manufactured. Inert lumps incapable of working newness, they were created, they are not creators.

> Some pour out gold from their bags
>> and weigh out silver on the scales;
> they hire a goldsmith to make it into a god,
>> and they bow down and worship it.
> They lift it to their shoulders and carry it;
>> they set it up in its place, and there it stands.
>> From that spot it cannot move.
> Though one cries out to it, it does not answer;
>> it cannot save them from their troubles.
>
> Isaiah 46:6,7

If the gods of the Babylonian empire are that impotent, so in the end is the empire impotent to save itself. Only God has the power for new life expressed in his promises.

To his religious criticism Isaiah adds a political critique against Babylon's merciless treatment of subjugated nations, thereby violating God's mandate:

> . . . I gave [my people] into your hand,
>   and you showed them no mercy.
> Even on the aged
>   you laid a very heavy yoke.
> You said, 'I will continue for ever –
>   the eternal queen!'
> But you did not consider these things
>   or reflect on what might happen.

Isaiah 47:6,7

Thus the continuation of the Babylonian empire depends upon its merciful treatment of others. God will call it to account for its cruelty.

We must pray that the church will be as willing to challenge the prevailing gods in our society, exposing their inability to deliver life and fulfilment, without appearing monotonously negative:

> The Christian style of life is marked by an extraordinary combination of detachment and concern. The Christian will care less for the world and, at the same time, care more for it than the person who is not a Christian. He will not lose his heart to it, but he may well lose his life for it.[3]

Be enthroned in the lives of your people, Lord, against the seductions of the new paganism. Empower us to expose the emptiness of current 'gods' with the courage and wit Isaiah showed when dealing with Bel and Nebo.

3. Practise radical promises

In our fight against tendencies to assimilate and despair in our time of exile, we should emulate Isaiah's call to captive Israel to go on the offensive and live by God's promises. The empire claimed to have the answers to its people's every requirement; they had no need to look outside the boundaries of the empire when everything was provided for within. How very similar that sounds to the claims of our own superstore culture. Notice how the political parties speak in terms of all-sufficiency. Isaiah doesn't deny that the empire meets many needs. But he asks the exiles to see the gifts which are beyond the power of the empire to give:

> 'Sing, O barren woman,
>   you who never bore a child;
> burst into song, shout for joy,
>   you who were never in labour;
> because more are the children of the desolate woman
>   than of her who has a husband,' says the LORD.
> 'Enlarge the place of your tent,
>   stretch your tent curtains wide,
>   do not hold back;
> lengthen your cords,
>   strengthen your stakes.
> For you will spread out to the right and to the left . . .'
>
> Isaiah 54:1–3

Exiles must choose: either they take the appearance of things as truth, or they dare to interpret life and look into the future through the lens of these unreasonable and audacious words. They had no trouble attributing names to Isaiah's cryptic references. The 'barren woman' was, of course, Sarah, but also captive Israel, 'the desolate woman'. 'Her who has a husband' was first, Hagar, but also Babylon – flourishing, glamorous, successful Babylon.

177

The prophecy turns the historical reality on its head. 'The barren woman', the old lady Sarah, and the captive Israel now sing and dance for joy, because they will swarm with children, far too many for their tent-home to contain. Everywhere the despised, defeated people of God are overflowing with new life and blessing which burst through all boundaries.

In speaking like this, Isaiah is subverting the present order, which always places the Babylonian empires on top and power-less, defeated people (and the church) at the bottom. Babylon, however, is childless and it is the exiles who are bursting with young life! Isaiah reminds exiles of another way mapped out by the promises of God. So, too, for the church when she is slipping into a resigned pessimism over prospects for change, growth and new things. Appearances can indeed provoke a sense of hopelessness and exhaustion as we try to tinker away at the edges of things to improve the situation. But Isaiah's vision calls us out to sing and dance against the appearance of things, and to worship the living God who even now is ' making everything new' (Revelation 21:5).

Who can say at what levels those radical promises of life and overflowing blessing will be fulfilled in our own time? Do such promises bother market forces or the political systems, the CBI or the TUC, the millionaires club? Probably not. That is entirely within God's wisdom. What we do dare to ask, at least, is that the Christian congregations which pepper the landscape and the cityscape, will each in its own way enact Isaiah's stunning prophecy by fully trusting those outrageous and unreasonable promises of life for our barrenness, when the ones who were last will be the first.

Holy Father, you have called us to live for you in perplexing times which can feel like exile, even captivity. Cause your promises given through Isaiah to come good in our own churches. Raise the faith of your people to see marvellous new possibilities of fruitfulness where there is now barrenness, and joy where there is the gloom of despair and the failure of assimilation.

Questions for reflection and discussion

1. Do you agree that 'the exile' is the lens which best brings our present situation into focus, and directs prayer for the church in the world?
2. Check the 'health' of your own church against 'ten good reasons' (p 170, 171). Use your findings as a guide for intercession and ministry.
3. 'The church is called to live in the tension of being, at the same time called out of the world and sent into the world' (p 170). What in practice does this mean? Similarly, 'the Christian style of life is marked by an extraordinary combination of detachment and concern' (p 176). Detached from what? Concerned about what?
4. 'Neither a secularist church . . . nor a separatist church' (p 171). Does the church in our society err on one side or the other, or would you say it's rightly balanced?

Chapter 18

MAKE READY TO GO

Israel's seventy-year captivity in Babylon is our master analogy for prayer for our churches. We recognise the spiritual similarities between the challenges and the choices facing them in a strange land, and our own situation. The uncanny sense we have of being exiles in our own country, like resident aliens who belong somewhere else, reflects Israel's struggle. The host secularism in our own society is powerful and persuasive enough to put churches on the defensive, prone to assimilate, and even to despair secretly of ever knowing the power of the Lord.

Support for these observations arrives in the latest survey of growth and decline (and the reasons for each) in British churches.[1] A year-long study of 14,000 church goers and those who have left reveals 'a widespread sense of anger and frustration' at what is perceived to be happening in churches in the UK and Ireland. 'Excessive liberalism and lack of conviction' is blamed for decline in congregations and loss of a strong Christian distinctiveness suggesting a too cosy relationship with the spirit of the age (our 'Babylon'). You will recognise the signs: an uncritical open-mindedness on the part of Christians towards a culture where the-newest-is-the-truest, and the-latest-is-the-greatest; an obsession with a dubious 'relevance'; embarrassment at the non-negotiable character of divine revelation and Christ's transcendent authority as the only Saviour of the world. Such attitudes are indications that these exiles have lost their way in the back alleys of Babylon.

We are discovering in Isaiah's word to his 'church in captivity' (chapters 40–55) directions for our prayer 'for all the saints'.

180

In the previous chapter we looked at three of the prophet's messages in which he called on captive Israel to disentangle their minds from Babylonian seductions, to embrace their Jewish difference, and to examine their attitudes in preparation for the Lord's next move. Have no doubt, he is at the door but 'when he comes will he find faith on earth?' To summarise, we saw that, when applied to ourselves, Isaiah's words call for the following responses:

1. Clarity and alertness

Pray for clarity in the minds of our churches; a clear sight of how 'Babylon' impinges on our faith; be alert to the conforming pressures of secularism; pray for an urgent desire to return to our spiritual origins, to rediscover our primitive, unique faith-memories of a crucified God bursting from the grave for the world's salvation.

2. Captivated by the gospel

Pray for Christian hearts and minds to be captivated, all over again, by the gospel. Pray for our congregations to be so convinced of Christ and delighted with him that they will dare to criticise the prevailing Babylon, its gods, its goals, and its demise under God's judgement. Pray for a fearless, intelligent response to Babylonian delusion, an evangelism that reaches to the heart of the culture.

3. Dare to live by God's promises

Pray that 'all the saints' will dare to live by God's marvellous promises of new life, boundlessly overflowing to discouraged exiles, promises of incredible fruitfulness for 'the barren . . . the desolate.'

One man, at least, resisted Babylon by the way he prayed, and thereby initiated Israel's tradition of 'the three hours of prayer' (see chapter 7). Daniel rejected King Darius' edict that all prayer must be directed to him (Daniel 6:6–13): '. . . Three times a day he got down on his knees and prayed, giving thanks to his God . . .' (v 10). By the very act of praying we are able to prove, at least to ourselves, that we are seeing the world Christ's way and not as Babylon sees it.

We are now ready for Isaiah's three further messages.

4. 'Sing to the Lord a new song'

The prophet turns exiles into subversive revolutionaries as they sing of a fundamentally different reality, beyond Babylon's grasp. Against all reasonable expectation they discover that they can 'sing the songs of the Lord while in a foreign land' (Psalm 137:4), not simply nostalgic songs about Jerusalem, nor songs of resignation, but a new story about their God coming to break Babylon's cruel grasp on the nations, a song about God's new order, a gospel song:

> Sing to the LORD a new song,
>> his praise from the ends of the earth,
> you who go down to the sea, and all that is in it,
>> you islands, and all who live in them.
> Let the desert and its towns raise their voices;
>> let the settlements where Kedar lives rejoice.
> Let the people of Sela sing for joy;
>> let them shout from the mountain tops.
> Let them give glory to the LORD
>> and proclaim his praise in the islands.

Isaiah 42:10–12

What an extraordinary pastor Isaiah was! We would expect him to speak in a gentle, consoling voice to his displaced people. Instead he teaches them a song which, in the Lord's name, lays claim to the world around Babylon. That world, as much as Israel, is the subject of the new song. It reaches out to include everyone, every-

182

thing, everywhere! In a word, whatever exists, whatever draws breath, does so in order to 'give glory to the LORD' (v 12).

The new song arises in the hearts of exiles at the coming of their divine deliverer. It sweeps over the seas, coastlines, islands, villages, empty deserts and teeming cities, the hills and the mountains, calling on all things to repeat the song of God's transforming grace. Glance once more at George Herbert's sonnet 'Prayer', (page 136, line 8), where prayer is described as 'a kind of tune, which all things hear and fear'. It is the exile's new song, and a fascinating image of the power of a church when open to God's purpose.

If you wonder if you are in danger of drifting into compromise and assimilation with 'Babylon', here is a simple check: How is your singing? What are you singing?

We will pray that 'all the saints' will be renewed in worship, singing the new song of confidence in the Lord who is in the affairs of the nations, drawing all things his way:

> The LORD will march out like a champion,
> like a warrior he will stir up his zeal;
> with a shout he will raise the battle cry
> and will triumph over his enemies.

Isaiah 42:13

And if the Lord as fighting man conjures up too many images of carnage, read on to Isaiah's next metaphor of unstoppable power:

> For a long time I have kept silent,
> I have been quiet and held myself back.
> But now, like a woman in childbirth,
> I cry out, I gasp and pant.

Isaiah 42:14

There is no more creative, life-giving 'violence' than childbirth. New life where there was no life. The Lord comes, and all things are born again. Expect transformations:

183

> I will lead the blind by ways they have not known,
> along unfamiliar paths I will guide them;
> I will turn the darkness into light before them
> and make the rough places smooth.
> These are the things I will do;
> I will not forsake them.

Isaiah 42:16

Every declaration of the Lord's intention ('I will . . . I will . . . I will') is in the same breath a judgement upon Babylon's idols who 'cannot'. Whenever we name and adore the Lord in our new, imperialistic song of his overcoming grace, some other impostor is dethroned. And we, in our place and time, in our embattled churches, can sing such a song because we know what the world doesn't know:

> No, in all these things we are more than conquerors through him who loved us. For I am convinced that neither death nor life, neither angels nor demons, neither the present nor the future, nor any powers, neither height nor depth, nor anything else in all creation, will be able to separate us from the love of God that is in Christ Jesus our Lord.

Romans 8:37–39

Our best songs and hymns will be those which, in some form and arrangement or another, set Paul's revelations to music. And in the experience of the church, 'new songs' have been the catalyst for new things. How many Christians have discovered themselves agreeing with the Lord to undertake risky endeavours, in the act of singing, say, Charles Wesley's hymn,

> Give me the faith that can remove
> and sink the mountains to the plain.

and in daring to ask for no less than 'a thousand tongues' to sing our great redeemer's praise?

Another mark of the authentic new song, sung by captives, is joy. Always, in some form, it celebrates and ponders emancipation through Christ's resurrection. Patrick Kavanagh called the resurrection:

> . . . a laugh freed
> forever and forever.[2]

Lord, pour into the hearts of your people the joy and laughter of the resurrection, the joy that you have released by your mighty power and nothing in heaven or earth can reverse. Whether by new gifts of composition or through the revitalising of our older hymns, in this gloomy, anxious age, bless your people with a new spirit of glad worship.

Christians who have believed joyously through terrible trials speak to us with special authority. When Pastor Bonhoeffer was in a Nazi cell awaiting execution he wrote to a relative 'Keep well, enjoy the beautiful country, spread *hilaritas* – "cheerfulness" – around you and keep it yourself too', and went on to suggest that music would 'keep a ground-base of joy alive in you'. Professor Ford comments: 'Bonhoeffer's way is of constantly renewed recognition of God in all the complexities and agonies of living, and an accompanying liberation from concern for oneself. Maturity is faithfulness according to one's situation and gifts, the willingness to focus afresh on the presence of God here and now. The death and resurrection of Jesus Christ is the ultimate standpoint for Christian praise.'[3] Or, as we have been trying to say, live the 'new song'.

As Isaiah approaches the conclusion of his 'messages of preparation' for exiles he has some advice about rations.

5. Choose wisely – eat well

He who supplies our daily food earns our allegiance. In place of Babylonian junk food, the Lord offers extraordinary fare for exiles on the move:

Come, all you who are thirsty,
    come to the waters;
and you who have no money,
    come, buy and eat!
Come, buy wine and milk
    without money and without cost.
Why spend money on what is not bread,
    and your labour on what does not satisfy?
Listen, listen to me, and eat what is good,
    and your soul will delight in the richest of fare.

Isaiah 55:1,2

It matters that we eat, and what we eat. The current near-hysteria about the harm done to us by excessive use of additives in our food confirms the point that we are what we eat. Israel had a unique history of being fed by the hands of tyrants: Pharaoh in the time of their Egyptian captivity and now other totalitarian rulers in Babylon. Isaiah's message takes up the experience of eating at the ovens of Egypt, thereby becoming slaves dependent on Pharaoh. Two months down the road from Egypt to Canaan came their first food crisis (Exodus 16), when many wanted to return to the land of slavery because, '. . . There we sat round pots of meat and ate all the food we wanted' (v 3). Anything, even servitude, is better than starvation. Then God gave another sort of food, an alternative bread supply from heaven, manna, 'the grain of heaven. Human beings ate the bread of angels; he sent them all the food they could eat' (Psalm 78:24,25). God earned the right to be Israel's God by feeding them.

Imprinted on Israel early in their existence was the principle that there is no need to submit to any Pharaoh in order to eat. The same principle was reaffirmed in the wonderful story of Daniel (see Daniel 1) when he and other promising young men in Babylonian captivity were chosen for special training and a bright future. 'The king assigned them a daily amount of food and wine from the king's table. . . .' (v 5) – but the young Jews chose instead to eat the 'diet of faithfulness' – vegetables. Daniel and his companion brilliantly outperformed the others who ate the rich royal food.

Isaiah draws on memories such as these to demonstrate to the exiles that there is a source of nourishment beyond the scope of Pharaoh's chefs, and Nebuchadnezzar's bakeries. Food is essential: reject the seductive fare of Egypt and Babylon and feast at the Lord's table – incredible food and all free! It raises the question of why anyone would choose to go to the same restaurant day after day, for meals which leave one unsatisfied and unnourished, fed with beautifully packaged and skilfully marketed junk food. If the empire's food is valueless, then be done with it. Imperial bread will make you ill, it is the bread of affliction, the dubious 'reward' given by the empire to those who do her work as slaves.

Spiritual eating disorders abound, and Christians must demonstrate before society that in Jesus we have an alternative food supply, which satisfies and builds up. Each time we come to the Holy Communion table to receive Christ's broken bread and outpoured wine, we are saying (to ourselves, to one another, to the world and to the Lord) that he alone nourishes. At that moment we reject the rubbish food of godless ideology, the gospel of consumerism and security, a life with all risks removed.

We are surrounded by people who are discovering for themselves, and often at high speed, the debilitating effects of the spiritual diet on offer in society. It is a diet directed towards 'felt needs', which turn out too often to be false needs, 'needs' generated by current fashions in the culture. True needs, true hunger and thirst are a first step towards faith and prayer; bogus needs are the opposite and will lead the unwary towards disaster. 'That need which is no need, is a demon sucking at the spring of your life.'[4]

Christians will want to pray disillusioned hungry seekers into Christ's banquet.

6. It's time to go

Isaiah's sixth and last message to exiles is preparation for
exodus into liberty. We are a people with unique roots in Christ
crucified and risen; we dare to unmask the illusory claims of
secularism; we have a new song in our hearts; we live by God's
astonishing promises; we eat the Lord's food. And now we are
ready to live the life God has set us to live in the world. It is time
to 'leave', even while, physically and literally, we continue living
in this world:

> Depart, depart, go out from there!
>   Touch no unclean thing!
> Come out from it and be pure,
>   you who carry the vessels of the LORD.
> But you will not leave in haste
>   or go in flight;
> for the LORD will go before you,
>   the God of Israel will be your rear guard.
>
> Isaiah 52:11,12

We are called to learn how to 'depart' from Babylon even though
we must, in the present life, continue to live in her streets. It
means, for the church, that we are disentangling ourselves, in our
attitudes, motivations and patterns of life and ministry, from the
mind of the world. In a word, a familiar word, depart from
'assimilation' with the Babylonian mind. We may take one
example of the danger we are in from Os Guinness' book *Dining
with the Devil*. He is responding to a statement which is, he says,
nothing short of canonical in the church-growth movement that
a fundamental principle of Christian communication is 'the
audience, not the message, is sovereign.'

Os Guinness comments that 'while many people still appear
moonstruck by the recent discovery of the sovereign audience, it
is worth pondering a *New Yorker* lament, about what is lost in
the brave, new, "audience-driven" preaching of the day: "The

preacher, instead of looking out upon the world, looks out upon public opinion, trying to find out what the public would like to hear. Then he tries his best to duplicate that, and bring his finished product into a marketplace in which others are trying to do the same. The public, turning to our culture to find out about the world, discovers that there is nothing but its own reflection. The unexamined world, meanwhile, drifts blindly into the future." '5

This return from Babylon echoes the earlier one at the Exodus, except that in Exodus the people dropped everything and ran out of Egypt as fast as they could go. This time, in contrast, they (we) are specifically instructed not to leave in haste because 'the Lord will go with you'. The message concludes:

> You will go out in joy
>   and be led forth in peace;
> the mountains and the hills
>   will burst into song before you,
> and all the trees of the field
>   will clap their hands.

Isaiah 55:12

Protected on every side from attack by marauding Babylonian troops, we make our way calmly, even serenely. People in Babylon watching our progress will be impressed by the absence of panic, for we sing and our children play as we go, and the elderly can go at their own pace. Observers will remark that these people seem to know what is going on, they travel with a certain mastery over circumstances because the Lord leads the way.

All creation sees and rejoices with returning exiles, 'mountains and trees', those symbols of creation's age and wisdom, can see in our demeanour the great sign 'that the creation itself will be liberated from its bondage to decay and brought into the glorious freedom of the children of God' (Romans 8:21). Therefore, by coming out of the spiritual system we have called 'Babylon', we are at the same time a pledge to the world that it has a future in God's new work.

Holy Father, call your people, the church, to know you and to bear faithful witness to you in this world. By your Holy Spirit make us a grateful, praising people; feed us with the life of your Son, our heavenly manna; enable us to go with you towards our eternal home, to travel in such a manner, and with such a style, that many Babylonians will be drawn to come with us.

Finally . . .

We can picture captive Jews gathering in their meetings to hear Isaiah's messages read. How did they respond to the prophet's words of challenge and encouragement? We have noticed before the dynamic and imaginative style of Israelite worship (p 71) and it's difficult to believe that they would have confined their interests to 'discussion groups'! Drama, dance, composition of poems and songs, tears and feasting, all would have played a part in the exile's vivid enactment of the message.

What impact will we allow Isaiah's words to have on our own worship? Such celebrations and enactments will take place on Sundays in church but their knock-on effect will be seen in changed attitudes towards society, economics, politics and education in our Monday-to-Saturday life.

Holy Spirit, make your people glad, very glad at the wonderful things you say to us, and promise us, through Isaiah. Set our hearts on fire with love for your love. Be pleased to accept our worship.

Questions for reflection and discussion

1. We seem to be receiving mixed messages: on the one hand we hear that Christian love requires a non-judgemental, inclusive attitude towards society; but the lessons of the Captivity demand that we defend our Christian distinctiveness. Look again at p 180 and discuss how we might reconcile the two apparently conflicting demands.
2. At this point you may want to pause and take up the prayer pointers on p 170,171.

3. 'Sing to the Lord a new song' (p 182). Paraphrase Isaiah's song to fit your own circumstances. For example:

 . . . You will travel to work each day,

you children and students off to school,

you shopping mall and all in the high street

etc etc.

 . . . let them shout from the housing estates.

4. Reflect on the observation that in fact there is no 'new *song*', since the song of God's deliverance (from Exodus to Pentecost) is essentially one and the same. But each time new *singers*.

5. Consider the suggestion that God's redeemed people journey 'calmly, even serenely. . . . [with an] absence of panic . . .. they travel with a certain mastery over circumstances' (p 189). Would you say that we convey such an impression, or do we appear as harassed and as insecure as the rest of society?

Chapter 19

THE WORK OF A PERFUMER

A vision of angels playing with fire opened this book (p 15,16). In conclusion, we will take a second glimpse at that event.

> Another angel, who had a golden censer, came and stood at the altar. He was given much incense to offer, with the prayers of all the saints, on the golden altar before the throne. The smoke of the incense, together with the prayers of the saints, went up before God from the angel's hand. Then the angel took the censer, filled it with fire from the altar, and hurled it on the earth; and there came peals of thunder, rumblings, flashes of lightning and an earthquake.
>
> Revelation 8:3–5

God bestows an infinite number of things on the world without our asking: '. . . He causes his sun to rise on the evil and the good, and sends rain on the righteous and the unrighteous' (Matthew 5:45). However, it seems that he gives 'fire on the earth' when the prayers of his people reach his presence like clouds of aromatic incense smoke. If, after all we have said about the power of prayer, we still need convincing, here is the last word: our prayers matter because God says they matter; he will have us crucially involved in the way he acts in the world. Never mind the 'whys?' and the 'what ifs?' and the 'buts'. God chooses to treat our commitment to his reign so seriously that he awaits our prayer before sending his conflagrations of judgement and salvation into the world.

The prayers of the church threaten and disturb the life of the world. Christians are the arsonists. Look at current affairs for evidence of 'thunder, rumblings, lightning and earthquakes.' The evening news on your television, the reports in your daily paper, are signs that Christians are praying. But most profoundly it is in the restlessness of the human heart and the unquiet conscience where we see the fire of God on earth, disturbing so as to lead people into peace. We do not pray for God's fire in order to torment our enemies, the bully-boy 'Babylonian' systems that are always with us in some form or other; rather we pray that the judge of all the earth will save his creation by burning off the dross of godlessness to leave what is true and good for the well-being of the human family.

Thus we have returned to incense-prayer in order to clinch in our minds the value of our prayers to God. Things are different because we pray. But look a little closer at the rich symbolism of incense as worship.

The aromas of prayer

Standing behind the vision of the great angel of Revelation pouring 'much incense' on the glowing coals of the altar of perfume, is Moses responding to the Lord's instructions for Israel's worship in the desert:

> Take the following fine spices . . . Make these into a sacred anointing oil, a fragrant blend, the work of a perfumer. . . . Take fragrant spices . . . and make a fragrant blend of incense, the work of a perfumer. . . .
>
> Exodus 30:23–25,34,35

Both oil and incense were for the Lord alone: both were rare (imported from the East; compare the Magi's offering, Matthew 2:11), hand-made, costly, pure, symbolic of the Lord's holy presence, distinctive and lovely aromatic scents perfuming the house of God, speaking of the beauty of holiness.

A man performs the work of a perfumer offering fragrant incense morning and evening in the middle of the desert. What is it for, what does it do? To the psalmist it was a symbol of spiritual fervour, 'May my prayer be set before you like incense' (Psalm 141:2), heart and mind wholly given up to God, ascending like the aromatic smoke. In the act of burning on the hot coals, the incense is transposed into another sphere, the invisible realm of the presence of God, and with it go the love and worship of our lives. For the rest of the day the worshipper will seek to live out in practice what he has enacted and proposed symbolically. He carries the evidence around with him, as anyone who has used incense will know; it infiltrates and permeates everything, like the effects of prayer.

Incense suggests 'pure' prayer, which we have mentioned before. It is an elusive aspect of worship, puzzling for those who practise a more pragmatic view of the Christian life – 'prayer in = blessings out'. 'Pure' prayer is worship offered for no other reason than to adore God, without ulterior motives and with no strings attached. There is even a touch of 'pointlessness' to such praying because it isn't 'necessary', it simply wants to glorify the Lord even though 'there is no need to' and 'there is nothing to be gained' from doing so. Incense is a symbol of prayer as a response to God's self-giving love. In 'pure' prayer we attempt (however inadequately) to make a sincere answer to the Lord in order to show him that we have understood him. He desires in us what every true lover desires, which is for the beloved to understand what he is saying. Love seeks no other reward than love in return.

Incense is, of course, not itself that pure answering prayer, but its symbol. We have an altar, in our own mind, an altar of incense (or perfume) in our deepest interior life, from which place we fulfil the command to 'pray continually' (1 Thessalonians 5:17). When incense-prayer becomes the routine instinct of the inner life, deeper than deliberate thought, beyond words, unceasingly and largely unselfconsciously, the heart breathes its adoration in the Spirit, trusting that 'he who searches our hearts knows the mind of the Spirit' (Romans 8:27).

Like the original altar in the desert tabernacle, the altar of incense in the heart must also be tended, morning and night (Exodus 30:7,8). Ash accumulates, and if it is left it smothers the glowing coals; it must be regularly raked out by self-examination, confession of sin, and the re-setting of the heart towards God by a simple prayer for light and fire:

> *As we rejoice in the gift of this new day,*
> *so may the light of your presence, O God,*
> *set our hearts on fire with love for you;*
> *now and for ever. Amen*[1]

Beautiful, beautiful, beautiful God

Standing within the atmosphere of the tabernacle's aromatic fragrances, a thoughtful worshipper might wonder, 'What is my God like, to use oil and incense to teach me his presence?' Exquisite symbols, known through the body, felt on the skin, delighting the senses, lifting the spirits and calming the mind, welcoming and hopeful, they speak of the gladness, richness and beauty of God's holy presence. It is, of course, the same holy presence of God *outside* the tabernacle in '*ordinary*' creation. Oil, incense and tabernacle simply dramatise the truth we would otherwise so easily forget. 'All things' are Christ's, and are upheld in being and beauty by his wisdom and power. 'All things' constitute his tabernacle; the aromas of his presence are in 'all things'.

The personal loss and sadness of practical *un*holiness in our lives is felt in its dull emptiness, bereft of the fragrance of God's beautiful presence. Incense speaks of the beauty of the Lord, it is the first impression made on the worshipper entering the tabernacle – 'my God is different and he is beautiful.' How strange and perverse of us that we should ever find prayer a struggle when coming to the beautiful God; Hopkins called him 'beauty's self and beauty's giver'. At the conclusion of this book, it is surely most appropriate that we should allow ourselves to do that too rare thing, to wander into the beauty of God, and discover for ourselves that prayer is a conversation with 'beauty's self and beauty's giver'. Like the scent of incense on clothes, such prayer has its own aromas.

Mostly anonymous performers

The poet Patrick Kavanagh was fascinated with how God may hide his ravishing loveliness in creation in the most out-of-the-way, neglected, unglamorous places, such as the far corner of an Irish bog – a sign of the breathtaking generosity of God's beauty.

THE ONE

> Green, blue, yellow and red –
> God is down in the swamps and marshes
> Sensational as April and almost incredible the flowering of
>   our catharsis.
> A humble scene in a backward place
> Where no one important ever looked
> The raving flowers looked up in the face
> Of the One and the Endless, the mind that has baulked
> The profoundest of mortals. A primrose, a violet,
> A violent wild iris – but mostly anonymous performers
> Yet an important occasion as the Muse at her toilet
> Prepared to inform the local farmers
> That beautiful, beautiful, beautiful God
> Was breathing his love by a cut-away bog.[2]

If we would do 'the work of a perfumer' we must acquire skill in looking for, and discerning, the presence of the 'beautiful, beautiful, beautiful God' wherever it is manifested. It will require our senses, those 'talismans of the Lord' to be in good shape for this work of seeing, hearing, feeling, tasting, smelling.

Our senses are under continuous bombardment, sometimes crude and coarsening, but equally dangerous when subtle and sophisticated – defiling, corrupting, desensitising as we pass through an average day. The cult of ugliness flourishes (if that is the word!) on every hand. When Richard Cook, the art critic, visited the 49th Venice Biennale, he was struck by the wilful gloom and ugliness of much of the exhibition. He writes:

The Italian Pavilion contains several other unfamiliar artists. Ene-Liis Semper, a young newcomer from Estonia, plays a dejected, crop-haired woman in a grainy black-and-white video installation called FF/REW. After reading disconsolately at a table, she gets up, puts a noose around her neck, and kicks away the stool supporting her feet. Respite is offered as the footage goes into reverse, taking her back to the table. But then she attempts another suicide with a gun, and finally succeeds in hanging herself again.[3]

Despair and ugliness are in the mainstream. They are institutionalised, adored and generously bankrolled. They infiltrate our environment wall-to-wall, and this in a world belonging to 'beauty's self and beauty's giver'. Anyone wishing to do the work of a perfumer will attend to what is happening to their senses as much as to their intellect. Keep those senses cleansed, sensitive and educated in the Lord's beauty: '. . . Whatever is true, whatever is noble, whatever is right, whatever is pure, whatever is lovely . . . think about such things' (Philippians 4:8).

What do I love in loving you?

It is a common complaint that our head and heart compete for control of our prayer–life, which divides between intellect and feeling, our thought and our emotions. If there is a bias in Evangelical spirituality, it is possibly towards brainwork, 'proof' and knowledge. Even as we are in the act of praying, something in the back of our head is monitoring and analysing the process. How we envy those exuberant African Christians throwing themselves unselfconsciously into their song, chant and dance! A 'perfumer' appointed to the work of prayer, will engage his senses, in company with hard thinking, both ascending together like the aromatic incense. The great Augustine (AD 354–430) gives a beautiful description of his 'mind-and-heart' approach to the 'beautiful, beautiful, beautiful God'.

Fuelling the Fire

When I love God

My love of you,
O Lord,
is not some vague feeling:
it is positive and certain.
Your word struck into my heart
and from that moment I loved you.
Besides this, all about me,
heaven and earth
and all that they contain
proclaim that I should love you,
and their message never ceases
to sound in the ears of all mankind,
so that there is no excuse for any
not to love you . . .
But what do I do when I love my God?
not material beauty
or beauty of a temporal order;
not the beauty of a temporal light,
so welcome to our eyes;
not the sweet melody of harmony and song;
not the fragrance of flowers,
perfumes and spices;
not manna or honey;
not limbs such as the body delights to embrace.
It is not these that I love when I love my God.
And yet, when I love him
it is true that I love a light of a certain kind,
a voice, a perfume, a food, an embrace;
but they are of the kind that I love in
my inner self,
when my soul is bathed in light
that is not bound by space;

When it listens to sound that never dies away;
When it breathes fragrance
That is not borne away on the wind;
when it tastes food
that is never consumed by the eating;
when it clings to an embrace from which
it is not severed by fulfilment of desire.
That is what I love
when I love my God.[4]

The picture of the praying, worshipping, ministering church as a priest performing 'the work of the perfumer' is a beautiful response to our beautiful Lord. If received and practised it would transform our worship and witness with the sheer joy of it. Our Lord Jesus fills the house of the cosmos with the ravishing incense of his praise to the Almighty Father, in the Holy Spirit, drawing our own prayer up into his, and answering with 'fire on earth' (Revelation 8:3–5).

Worship as 'the aromas of love' is a rich theme. In the tabernacle, it was the lovely aromas of oil and incense. When Mary poured her 'expensive perfume' (John 12:3) over Jesus' feet, and then broke all the taboos by 'wiping his feet with her hair', the work of that perfumer was inspired by grateful love. All four gospels give accounts of a woman anointing Jesus. In Luke (Luke 7:36–50), she wet the Lord's feet with her tears, then wiped them with her hair, kissed them and anointed them. Jesus traced that extraordinary display to her 'great love'. In John's account, the effect of Mary's costly devotion was that, as a side effect, 'the house was filled with the fragrance of the perfume' (v 3). It appears that the essential qualification for anyone who would do 'the work of a perfumer' is a heart overflowing with grateful love. Where does that leave those of us who, in spite of our orthodox faith, are aware of a certain hardness of heart, light years away from the all-consuming, grateful love of those women?

The Holy Spirit comes to the aid of our failed worship. Urs Balthasar writes: 'To him [the Holy Spirit] we must open ourselves up, without defensiveness, without thinking that we know better, without hardening ourselves, so that we may undergo initiation by him into the mystery that God is love. Let us not imagine that we already know this ourselves! "This is love: not that we loved God, but that he loved us and sent his Son as an atoning sacrifice for our sins" (1 John 4:10). The Spirit alone teaches us this reversal of perspective, but through him we can really learn what, in his view, love is.'[5] We tend the altar of incense in the heart, but only the Holy Spirit can set the coals glowing.

The 'oriental fragrancy' of worship

Once into this theme of prayer as the 'work of the perfumer' our thought is led in surprising directions. If you will glance once more at George Herbert's sonnet (p 136), in the last line he refers to prayer as 'the land of spices' recalling the descriptions of incense and oil in the tabernacle (Exodus 30:23,34,35). He also gives the metaphor of prayer as perfume a startling turn, when he describes the Lord Jesus as an 'oriental fragrancy'. Herbert believed that the best defence against the creeping paralysis of spiritual dryness, when the heart hardens into sterile formality and barrenness, was to plunge his mind into the 'oriental fragrancy' of the two words 'My Master'.

How sweetly doth *My Master* sound! *My Master*!

As Ambergris leaves a rich scent
unto the taster:
So do these words a sweet content,
and oriental fragrancy, *My Master.*

With these all day I do perfume my mind,
my mind even thrust into them both.[6]

We have arrived finally at what is a wonderful picture of our communion with the Lord, beautiful in its simplicity. As we stand before him doing the work of a perfumer, our prayers ascend like incense into his presence. Once aromatic perfumes are out, there can be no stopping them: they invade every corner of the house. When the Holy Spirit chose to speak of prayer, under the image of incense ascending, he implied that our prayers perfume the very presence of God, giving him pleasure.

It is also true that the Lord Jesus – *My Master* – is like a perfume and when we daily thrust our mind into the unfathomable riches of those two words, their 'oriental fragrancy' permeates our interior world. Communion is the 'holy intoxication' of delighting God, and being delighted by him.

> *Blessed are you, Sovereign God of all,*
> *to you be glory and praise for ever!*
> *As we look for your coming among us this day,*
> *open our eyes to behold your presence*
> *and strengthen our hands to do your will,*
> *that the world may rejoice and give you praise,*
> *Father, Son and Holy Spirit.*[7]

Questions for reflection and discussion

There are several things in this final chapter worth taking up in further meditation and action:

1. 'Pure' prayer, the prayer which is our love's answer to God's love, prayer free from artificial motives, prayer which tells the Lord that, yes, we are beginning to understand what he is saying to us (p 194).
2. The perfumer's essential routine, am and pm, of raking over the ash accumulating in the heart's altar (p 194,195).
3. 'We should allow ourselves to do that too rare thing, to wander into the beauty of God, and discover for ourselves that prayer is conversation with "beauty's self and beauty's giver"' (p 195).

Fuelling the Fire

4. Look again at Augustine's testimony 'When I love God' (p 198,199). Over the next days, as a focus for your meditation, under the same heading with your own description of what your love for God is, and what it isn't.

REFERENCES AND SOURCES

Chapter 1 Coordinated with Eternity

1. Robert Brown, quoted in *Wisdom for the Way*, compiled by Gordon S Jackson, NavPress, 2000, p 122.
2. Gerard Manley Hopkins, Poem 155, *Poems of Gerard Manley Hopkins*, edited by WH Gardner and NH MacKenzie, OUP, 1970.
3. George Herbert, 'Dooms-day', *The Complete English Poems* edited by John Tobin, Penguin, 1991, p 176.
4. Augustine, *Confessions*, translated by RS Pine-Coffin, Penguin Classics, 1987, Book 1.1.
5. Gerard Manley Hopkins, Poem 31 ('God's Grandeur'), *Poems of Gerard Manley Hopkins*, edited by WH Gardner and NH MacKenzie, OUP, 1970.
6. John Donne, 'A Hymn to God in My Sickness', in *John Donne, The Complete English Poems*, Penguin Books, 1982, p 347.
7. Wallace Stevens, quoted in Seamus Heaney, *The Redress of Poetry*, Faber, 1995, p 1.
8. Helmut Thielieke, *Encounter with Spurgeon*, James Clarke, 1964, p 11.
9. CS Lewis, *Perelandra (Voyage to Venus)*, Pan Books, 1983, p 183.

Chapter 2 The Bonfire

1. Gerard Manley Hopkins, Poem 72, *Poems of Gerard Manley Hopkins*, edited by WH Gardner and NH MacKenzie, OUP, 1970.

2. Hans Urs Balthasar, *You Crown the Year with Goodness*, Ignatius Press, 1989, p 158.
3. Hans Urs Balthasar, *You Crown the Year with Goodness*, Ignatius Press, 1989, p 179.

Chapter 3 Praying the Doctrine

1. Austin Farrer, *Lord, I Believe*, Faith Press, 1958, p 9.
2. J Jeremias, *The Prayers of Jesus*, SCM, 1967, p 85.

Chapter 4 The Apprenticeship

1. John Calvin, quoted in Karl Barth, *Prayer and Preaching*, SCM, 1964, p 20.
2. George Herbert, 'Providence', verse 2, *The Complete English Poems*, edited by John Tobin, Penguin, 1991, p 108.
3. Poem 37, *Poems of Gerard Manley Hopkins*, edited by WH Gardner and NH MacKenzie, OUP, 1970, p 69.
4. Lawrence Kushner, *The Book of Words*, Jewish Light Publishing, 1993, p 19.
5. Christopher Smart, 'Jubilate Agno,' *The Collected Poems of Christopher Smart*, edited by Norman Callan, Routledge & Kegan Paul, 1949, chapter 19.50.
6. CEB Cranfield, *The Gospel according to St. Mark*, CUP, 1963, p 66.

Chapter 5 With Empty Hands

1. See Raymond Fung, *The Isaiah Vision*, WCC Publications, 1992.
2. George Herbert, quoted in *Wisdom for the Way*, compiled by Gordon S Jackson, NavPress, 2000, p 58.
3. Austin Farrer, *Said or Sung*, Faith Press, 1964, p 59,60.

Chapter 6 Against the Darkness

1. J Jeremias, *New Testament Theology*, volume 1, SCM, 1975, p 95.
2. Kate Muir, *Times Magazine*, 6 November 2004, p 9.

Chapter 7 Praying Christ's Way

1. Austin Farrer, *Interpretation and Belief*, SPCK, 1976, p 12,13.
2. David F Ford, *Jubilate*, DLT, 1984, p 39.
3. J Jeremias, *The Prayers of Jesus*, SCM, 1967, p 76.

Chapter 8 'Feed the gaping need of my senses'

1. Patrick Kavanagh, 'Canal Bank Walk', *The Compleat Poems*, The Goldsmith Press, 1992, p 294.
2. John Brown, quoted in *Wisdom for the Way*, compiled by Gordon S Jackson, NavPress, 2000, p 84.
3. Leonard Ravenhill in *Wisdom for the Way*, compiled by Gordon S Jackson, NavPress, 2000, p 85.
4. Otto Kaiser, *Isaiah 1–12*, Old Testament Library, SCM, 1972, p 79.
5. From *Hebrew Verse, Hekalot Hymns*, edited and translated by T Carni, Penguin, 1981, p 196.
6. From the hymn 'Eternal Light' by T Binney (1798–1874).

Chapter 9 Duet: The Child and the Diva

1. Patrick Kavanagh, from the poem, 'The Self-Slaved', *The Compleat Poems*, The Goldsmith Press, 1992, p 293.
2. CS Lewis, *Letters to Malcolm*, Geoffrey Bles, 1964, p 12.
3. TF Torrance, *The Mediation of Christ*, Paternoster Press, 1983, p 107.

Chapter 11 Praying the Covenant

1. Julian of Norwich, *Revelations of Divine Love*, translated by E Colledge and J Walsh (London, 1978), p 226.
2. Francis of Assisi. This version of 'A Song for Brother Sun' in *Celebrating Common Prayer*, Mowbrays, 1992, p 232.

Chapter 12 Contemplative Prayer: A Dazzling World

1. See Ronald Rolheiser, *The Shattered Lantern*, Hodder and Stoughton, 1994, especially chapters 1–3.
2. Rolheiser, p 26.
3. 'Aurora Leigh' (1857), book vii.
4. GK Chesterton, quoted in Rolheiser, p 141.
5. Thomas Traherne, *Kingdom of God*, p. 226 (a recently discovered set of Traherne's meditations.
6. Traherne, *Centuries*, The Faith Press, 1960, 1:34.
7. *Centuries*, 1:37.
8. *Centuries*, 2:67.
9. *Centuries*, 4:93.

Chapter 13 Contemplative Prayer: the Face of God

1. W Eichrodt, *The Theology of the Old Testament*, Volume 1, SCM, 1961, p 121.
2. Hans Urs Balthasar, *The Grain of Wheat*, Ignatius Press, 1995, p 3.
3. David Hay, *Religious Experience Today*, Mowbray, 1990, p 71.
4. Gerard Manley Hopkins, 'Poem 57', *Poems of Gerard Manley Hopkins*. Edited by WH Gardner and NH MacKenzie, OUP, 1970.
5. Stephen Prickett, *Words and the Word*, CUP, 1989, p 119–122.

Chapter 14 Meditative Prayer: 'The soul is dyed the colour of its leisure thought'.

1. Emperor Marcus Aurelius.
2. Stuart Holden, quoted in *Wisdom for the Way*, compiled by Gordon S Jackson, NavPress, 2000, p 178.
3. For a fuller reflection on the sonnet, see Dennis Lennon, *Turning the Diamond*, SPCK, 2002.
4. Lawrence Kushner, *The Book of Words*, Jewish Light Publishing, 1993, p 27,28.

5. Urs Balthasar, *The Grain of Wheat*, Ignatius Press, 1995, p 113.
6. Steven Rose, *The Making of Memory*, Bantam, 1993, p 1.
7. George Steiner, *Real Presences*, Faber, 1990, p 9.

Chapter 15 When God is Silent

1. Clarence Day, quoted in *Wisdom for the Way*, compiled by Gordon S Jackson, NavPress, 2000, p 122.
2. John Baillie, *Christian Devotion*, OUP, 1962, p 20.
3. John Baillie, *Christian Devotion*, OUP, 1962, p 21.
4. George Herbert, 'Perseverance', *The Complete English Poems*, edited by John Tobin, Penguin, 1991, p 192.
5. Samuel Taylor Coleridge, in *Coleridge's Notebooks*, edited by Seamus Perry, OUP, 2000, p 175.
6. Thomas Keating, quoted in *Wisdom for the Way*, compiled by Gordon S Jackson, NavPress, 2000, p 123.
7. Christopher Morley, quoted in *Still Waters, Deep Waters*, edited by Rowland Croucher, Lion Publishing, 1987, p 157.

Chapter 16 A Condoned Violence

1. Richard Chenevix Trench, quoted in *Wisdom for the Way*, compiled by Gordon S Jackson, NavPress, 2000, p 127.
2. AW Tozer, quoted in *Wisdom for the Way*, compiled by Gordon S Jackson, NavPress, 2000, p 127.
3. Charles Williams, *Descent into Hell*, Eerdmans, 1999, p 95–98.
4. George MacDonald, in CS Lewis, *An Anthology*, Geoffrey Bles, 1946, p 115.
5. Jacques Ellul, quoted in *Wisdom for the Way*, compiled by Gordon S Jackson, NavPress, 2000, p 123.
6. Sirach 43:30,31.
7. John Donne, in George Herbert, *The Complete English Poems*, edited by John Tobin, Penguin, 1991, p 347.
8. Austin Farrer, *Said or Sung*, The Faith Press, 1964, p 19.
9. Quoted in *The Vision of Piers Plowman*, translated by Terence Tiller, BBC, 1981, p 227.

Chapter 17 Praying in Babylon

1. See David J Bosch, *Transforming Mission*, Orbis, 1992, p 11.
2. With grateful acknowledgement to an address by Walter Brueggemann.
3. Attributed to Bishop John Robinson.

Chapter 18 Making Ready to Go

1. Reported in *The Times*, 5 March 2005.
2. Patrick Kavanagh, 'Lough Derg', in *The Complete Poems*, p 114.
3. David F Ford, in *Jubilate*, DLT, 1984, p 87.
4. George MacDonald, *Unspoken Sermons*, second series, Sunrise Books, 1989, p 38.
5. Os Guinness, *Dining with the Devil*, Baker Books, 1994, p 59.

Chapter 19 The Work of a Perfumer

1. *Celebrating Common Prayer*, Mowbrays, 1992, p 15.
2. Patrick Kavanagh, 'The One', in *The Complete Poems*, p 291.
3. Richard Cook, *The Times*, 14 June 2004.
4. Augustine, *Confessions*, translated by RS Pine-Coffin, Penguin, 1987, p 211,12.
5. Hans Urs Balthasar, *Credo: Mediations on the Apostles' Creed*, T & T Clark, 1990, p 76.
6. George Herbert, 'The Odour', in *The Complete English Poems*, edited by John Tobin, Penguin, 1991.
7. *Celebrating Common Prayer*, Mowbrays, 1992, p 63.